IN SEARCH OF THE
SUPERNATURAL

Also by Yvette Fielding and Ciarán O'Keeffe:

GHOST HUNTERS:
A Guide to Investigating the Paranormal

IN SEARCH OF THE SUPERNATURAL

YVETTE FIELDING
and CIARÁN O'KEEFFE

HODDER

First published in Great Britain in 2008 by Hodder & Stoughton
An Hachette Livre UK company

1

A CIP catalogue record for this title is available from the British Library

ISBN 978 0 340 89981 6

Typeset in Minion by Hewer text UK Ltd, Edinburgh

Printed and bound in the UK by
CPI Mackays, Chatham ME5 8TD

Hodder & Stoughton policy is to use papers that are natural,
renewable and recyclable products and made from wood grown
in sustainable forests. The logging and manufacturing
processes are expected to conform to the environmental
regulations of the country of origin.

Hodder & Stoughton Ltd
338 Euston Road
London NW1 3BH

www.hodder.co.uk

'Do not ask, Reader, how my blood ran cold and my voice choked up with fear. I cannot write it: this is a terror that cannot be told.'
—Dante, *Inferno* (Ninth Circle, Canto XXXIV)

CONTENTS

INTRODUCTION: Into the Unknown

Ghost stories have always been part of human life, in the form of tales around the campfire and scary thrills at Hallowe'en, and more recently as the subject of television programmes such as *The X Files*, popular fiction like the books of Stephen King, and scientific investigations. The Society for Psychical Research and TV programmes like our own *Most Haunted* have turned ghost-hunting into a process involving investigations, data-gathering, theories and experiments. These things are all geared towards answering the big question: do ghosts really exist?

There are of course cynics and believers in the mix, both eager to put forward their own theories in the hope of either proving or disproving the existence of ghosts. Theories such as: are ghosts purely psychological projections, to do with the common unconscious fear of death? Are they hallucinations? Are they departed spirits or visions and echoes of events in the past? Or are they just stories? In this book we consider and discuss all aspects of the subject of ghosts, something we are able to do because of our very different approaches and attitudes to ghost-hunting.

In many ways, the two of us are polar opposites! While Yvette doesn't claim to be psychic, she is highly sensitive to changes in atmosphere, moods, and strange sensory phenomena like unexplained noises and smells. Ciarán, with his background in science, particularly parapsychology, provides a balancing perspective; that of the sceptic, the scientist, always in search of new knowledge and acutely aware of the myriad possible rational explanations.

Two very different personalities and approaches then. But we do have one thing in common: we are both ghost-hunting addicts. We can never hear of a haunted location or mysterious phenomenon without wanting to go and experience it for ourselves, find out what's going on, soak up the atmosphere and draw our own conclusions. This book is the result of our latest searches – ghost hunts that have taken us to some strange and unexpected places and almost turned our hair white in the process!

In our first book together, *Ghost Hunters: A Guide to Investigating the Paranormal*, we introduced you to 'everyday' cases, representative of the kind that are commonly documented and investigated today, but for this book we wanted to delve into some cases from further back in history, cases that have layer upon layer of hidden stories and legends just waiting to be uncovered.

In Part One, we look back into the past at six locations in the United Kingdom; what these locations have in common, apart from their centuries of rich and colourful history, is that they boast a real hotchpotch of ghostly eyewitness accounts, from jarring auditory phenomena in a sixteenth-century mansion with a long history of heartbreak, to the spine-chilling apparition of a ghostly 'pale lady' in a Liverpool park; from an old library where books inexplicably appear, disappear, and 'fall' from their shelves, to a terrifying report of a grotesque hanging phantom in a network of dark and claustrophobic underground tunnels.

Our first investigation takes place in Dartford Library in Kent. Neither of us had ever investigated a library before, and Ciarán in particular has always dreamt of hunting ghosts in a location like this. Our next stop is Allerton Tower in Liverpool, an abandoned Gothic manor house that has long been believed to boast a resident Grey Lady spirit. Still in the Liverpool area, for our third case we venture underground into an intricate and mysterious network of tunnels and mazes, where witnesses report seeing ghostly apparitions emerging from the darkness. We continue the underground theme for our investigation of a cavern in Derbyshire's Peak District, a part of the country with a long and chilling history of the para-normal. And we head to Chester's Stanley Palace, allegedly the most haunted house in this ancient city. Drawn by Chester's age and its reputation for haunted-ness and unexplained events, both of us have wanted an opportunity to investigate it for a long time. Finally, for all those romantics out there, our last port of call in the UK is Hever Castle, with a history stretching back to the thirteenth century, a melancholy royal past and, according to plenty of contemporary eyewitness accounts, a ghostly present.

In Part Two we turn our sights to spooky happenings abroad. Britain obviously has a long tradition of haunt-ings, but what about France? Do they report seeing ghosts there? What is the French people's attitude to the possibility of the paranormal? We were intrigued and keen to learn more about what cultural differences there might be between French and British hauntings and the way the paranormal is viewed in these two countries.

We started at the Château du Pays Lauragais in the south of France, attracted by the strange stories that Ciarán managed to coax out of some initially reluctant locals. That and the fact that the château looks absolutely terrifying at night! Another castle, the derelict Château de Puilaurens, attracted us because it is the only Cathar castle out of approximately fifty in the area to boast reliably reported ghosts. There's even reference to its ghostly reputation in some of the French guidebooks to the area, which is otherwise pretty much unheard of in France. Our final case in France is Rennes le Château, which intrigued us. Not, strictly speaking, for paranormal-investigation reasons, but rather as an essential component of our ongoing research into an aspect of the infamous *Da Vinci Code* story.

After France we travel further afield, for a final investigation across the Atlantic in California. We visit the Winchester Mystery House, which, with its macabre and melancholy history, might just be the most intriguing of all our investigations. Not to mention the fact that we managed to capture some compelling EVP (Electronic Voice Phenomena). When we asked who was there, did we hear an answering spirit voice?

We hope you'll agree that we have really mixed up the investigations for this book, bringing back from the most haunted crevices of the world a veritable bubbling cauldron of paranormal spookiness and deep mystery to keep you spellbound and goosepimpled. So, if you are ready, find a comfortable chair, put your feet up, and prepare to join us on our journey into the unknown.

Warning: If you are of a nervous disposition, perhaps you should read this book in a well-lit room!

Investigative Techniques

If you have read our first book, *Ghost Hunters*, and recall the chapter on Investigative Techniques then feel free to skip the following section. Jump to page 31, where our first investigation begins. Before we start, some words on how paranormal investigators like us work, and with what equipment and resources. Take heed if you are planning an investigation of your own!

GENERAL GUIDELINES

Generally we don't encourage people without training or experience to conduct a paranormal investigation. Before you head off, camera in hand, to that haunted cemetery, it really is important that you have some idea of what you are doing, what you need, and what you can expect. Reading this book, and our first book *Ghost Hunters*, is a great start. We also recommend that you contact an established organisation in your local area for information and advice, and also join them on a workshop or investigation, rather than striking out on your own straight away. It's a good idea to get a feel for what you might be getting yourself into! It will also help you to be prepared for the fact that not every investigation makes for a thrilling and scary adventure.

Here are some general guidelines for conducting a paranormal investigation:

- Find out all you can about the history of the place and/or building you intend to investigate. Newspapers, local historians, the internet and books can all be helpful for finding both folklore and hard facts about the site.
- Gather as much evidence as you can about the haunting from witnesses and local residents. In many cases the most important aspect of an investigation is witness interviews, as the testimony of eyewitnesses often determines which direction the investigation will take.
- Prepare in advance for every interview. Be open-minded and considerate of the feelings and comfort of your witness at all times. Allow your witness to tell their story from beginning to end without interruption. Hold off questions until they have finished, and make sure those questions aren't leading ones. For example:

  Leading questions: Did you see a ghost? Were you terrified?

Open questions: What did you see? How did you feel?

- As you gather information for your investigation please remember this very important point: respect the privacy of the residents in the area.

- Bear in mind that an overnight investigation may not always be necessary. Don't jump into it before you've done some preliminary research. A simple explanation for a reported haunting experience may be found early on in an investigation, just through interviews or researching the history of the location.

- If the place you want to investigate is a private property it is essential that you get permission from the owners or residents. It's also wise to notify the police if you're going to be taking pictures in a public place, like a graveyard, in the small hours of the morning. If it's a public building like a hospital or school, you also need to get permission from the site owners or care-takers. Always bring ID with you so that if you are questioned by anyone you can prove who you are.

- Never go alone. This just makes sense. If you fall over and hurt yourself, or just get scared out of your wits, you will need someone there. And make sure you let someone know where you will be in case of emergency.

- The best times to investigate tend to be from 9 p.m. to 6 a.m. as these are the hours most associated with haunting. Although of course you can also get results during daylight hours. If you do plan to carry out your investigation at night, always check out the site in daylight first so that you are familiar with it. Look out for potentially dangerous areas and obstacles that you may not be able to see in the dark.

- No smoking, alcohol or drugs at an investigation, for obvious reasons.
- Don't wear perfume, cologne or anything else with a very noticeable scent. This is so that people don't mistake the smell for a paranormal occurrence; spirits are said to sometimes use scents to get our attention. The no-perfume rule applies to both indoor and outdoor investigations.

WHAT YOU NEED

We've divided the following information on equipment into two categories: the basics, and optional and advanced items. If you are going to treat yourself to some high-tech gadgets, it's important that you properly understand their function and use. Give yourself time to learn how to use them and practise using them until you feel comfortable.

Are the high-tech gadgets essential? Although they can be helpful, we warn against becoming dependent on equipment. As long as you have the basics, have done your research and accumulated knowledge, and are open-minded, you really have all that you need.

The Basics

These items are essential for use in any investigation. They are easy to find, affordable and can fit into a small bag. They are suitable for groups or investigators who just wish to 'capture' evidence, rather than thoroughly investigate and discount every possible rational explanation. They are also for those who don't have the finances to splash out on every gadget going.

- Business card or some other ID – anything that shows your name and contact information.
- Notebook and pens. Plans of the location, if available, are useful too, especially to pinpoint experiences.
- Two torches with extra batteries. It's also an excellent idea to tape a piece of red gel or cellophane over the lens to preserve your own and your fellow investigators' night vision. Also, some investigators prefer to use headset torches, to free up their hands for note-taking and carrying other equipment.
- Tape recorder with blank tapes: use a quality tape recorder and a separate external microphone. Good-quality, branded, type 1 normal-position tapes are the best by far, as well as being the only tape that the majority of portable recorders will take. Avoid using micro-cassette dictation type recorders as the quality of the audio is usually poor. Always use brand-new blank tapes; never record over old ones. Good-quality digital audio recorders

can also be used very successfully, but avoid models that do not allow the user to connect an external microphone or only record in MP3 format, as this encoding removes a lot of the audio information at the top and bottom of the frequency range. Models that record in .WAV or PCM format are much better.

- 35mm camera: nothing fancy, but with at least 400-speed film. Also good at night is 800-speed film but you will need to test your camera's flash strength to see which speed works best for you. For best results use black-and-white film. Infra-red film does exist, but it's difficult to buy and get it developed, so there's no need to worry about that. Always buy good-quality film. When you develop the photos let the processor know you want all the pictures developed, including any that they might think are bad ones.

- Digital camera. Many respected people in this field are adamantly against the use of digital cameras for ghost hunts or research. One reason is that there is no negative to look at to identify an anomaly, whereas 35mm negative can be useful for analysing photos more closely. Another is that digital pictures can easily be tampered with using image-editing software. We have always felt that digital cameras are useful, and we use them in our research. Analysis of any interesting photos must only be done on image copies, with the originals left untouched after you've transferred them to a storage drive. Many of the digital cameras around today are of high quality and capable of taking photos on a par with 35mm cameras, and some can also take photos in a limited infra-red light spectrum. Some even allow pictures to be taken using Nightshot IR in complete darkness. The ease with which you can store and analyse photos, and delete uninteresting ones, is an added bonus. Another advantage is the ability to follow an energy source or spirit on the move.

- Wristwatch: so you can log in your times of arrival and departure, and events.
- Thermometer: to detect changes in room temperature. Rapid temperature drops of ten degrees or more, with no discernible natural cause, are thought to suggest spirit presence. Some argue that the best thermometers to use are the old-fashioned mercury type, as they believe that digital ones can fail when electromagnetic fields are present, but mercury thermometers just don't react quickly enough to measure a rapid temperature drop. For accuracy we recommend an infra-red thermometer with laser pointer. Note: where the laser is pointed is where the temperature is measured – this style of thermometer is not appropriate for cold spots in mid-air.
- Compass: useful for navigation and also for picking up magnetic activity, as a compass will react to the magnetic or electrical stimuli that are often reported in haunted areas. Compasses can only respond to a magnetic stimulus, although magnetic fields can be generated from an electrical source.

- Chalk to mark areas.
- Labels to identify items.
- Talcum powder to put on the floor to detect movement. An alternative, and perhaps more accurate, method is to use motion detectors (see below).
- First-aid kit in case of accident or injury.
- Tape measure, ball of string and a pair of scissors to mark and measure areas.
- Binoculars can sometimes be useful.
- Motion detectors: to sense unseen movements. There are two main types of motion detector, the passive infra-red and the light beam barrier. Both types are best used to ensure that locations or trigger objects are not accidentally or intentionally tampered with.
- Jackets or other weather-appropriate clothes. It's just common sense, but if you are cold you are not at your best and your observation skills could suffer.
- Food and drinks (hot!) are also essential.

Advanced and Optional

The following items can be extremely helpful, but they are not essential. Remember, paranormal investigators were investigating hauntings and making great discoveries before most of these items were even invented. Before using any of these items in the field, make sure that you know how they work and what you are looking for. It is no use collecting readings or data if you cannot interpret them in a meaningful way. The inclusion of most of the environmental monitoring equipment is to ensure that a paranormal explanation is the most likely one. Think about it like this: If you have a checklist of natural explanations and at the bottom is a paranormal one, you need to tick off every natural one first before arriving at the conclusion that you have something paranormal. Being able to tick off all of the natural explanations by the equipment not having captured data to support them strengthens your argument for paranormal evidence.

- Video camcorders (tripod optional): an important instrument for an investigation. Unlike still cameras, they can give us constant visual and audio surveillance for review and observation after the investigation. The video cameras we use are equipped with infra-red capability. A video will show what is happening, the length of time over which the phenomenon occurs, the conditions surrounding the phenomenon, and possibly even the cause of it. Most modern digital video recorders can be directly connected to a PC or laptop for transfer of footage or even to use as a webcam with motion-detection software.
- Night-vision equipment: a light-amplification system that takes in any available light including IR (infra-red) and amplifies it many times to make it visible. Night-vision equipment cannot work in total darkness, hence the small IR illuminator that many people use for locations with zero light.

- Spot lights: small, battery-powered spot lights can really help when it comes to setting up and taking down equipment. They can be used to get a better view and for safety reasons.
- Headset communicators: when you have a team of people investigating, these are a good idea for staying in contact if you separate or spread out. The hand-held walkie-talkies are fine, but the headset communicators free up your hands for things like recording notes and using cameras.
- Geiger counter: reads the amount of ionising radiation in the air and on an object. There are levels of ionising radiation around us all the time, but on an investigation you will be looking for abnormal levels. They are available for around £150 and are very simple to use. In fact they are not much different from an EMF meter.
- The EMF meter (Electromagnetic Field): a valuable device for the modern paranormal investigator. With this instrument it is possible to measure and locate sources of electromagnetism. Common sources for household EM readings include such mundane objects as computer monitors, mobile telephones, bedside clock radios, and televisions. There are arguments both for and against using this type of meter. It has been suggested by some that spirits may disrupt the EMF within a location, or even emit their own EMF. Ciarán's view follows research being conducted in Canada and in the field in the UK. This research

suggests that particular levels of or minuscule fluctuations in the EMF can mildly stimulate a part of our brain that may then provoke a physiological reaction, or even a sensory hallucination in some individuals. Before using the EMF meter on an investigation, it is advisable to walk around the area and take initial readings around energy sources such as light poles or electrical outlets. Most units come with a manual describing the normal electromagnetic reading of household appliances. When using EMF meters it is important to make a series of baseline measurements in order to highlight any unusual readings. A normal range of readings is between 0.1 and 10mG, although we hesitate to use the word 'normal' really since some locations may have sources that are higher but are manmade. For example, if you are near a domestic appliance the reading can exceed 30mG. Most of the EMF meters on the market are hand-held, which is not ideal; it means that you must make sure you stand very still when using them. Moving around even a little can affect the readout slightly and, unless you know this, you may end up interpreting your data incorrectly. In an ideal world you would purchase a tri-axial EMF meter (3-axis) as opposed to the more common 1-axis variety. Both varieties have their uses in investigations, however, since a single-axis meter is generally a better tool for locating the source of an emission. Additionally, we use a 3-axis meter that can be left static and the data recorded on to its memory or fed directly into a computer – this removes the potential for human error.

- Infra-red thermal imager or scanner: can pinpoint abnormal cold or hot spots on solid surfaces. This is another device that must be tested before being used in the field. Be aware that IR thermal imagers can *only* detect hot and cold spots on solid surfaces, not cold spots in the air.
- Air ion counter: measures positive and negative ions in the atmosphere. Again, test before using, and look for abnormal readings during an investigation. Air ion counters quantify the numbers of air ions and indicate their charge. They are very difficult to use properly and require a great deal of care to avoid misleading information being obtained. We think that it may be best to drop the air ion counter in favour of the negative-ion detector (NID), which simply indicates when the amounts of negative air ions exceed normal levels. Increased negative ion amounts have been linked to increased reports of paranormal activity within some locations.

THE INVESTIGATION

Have everyone meet at the location, then decide who will work each piece of equipment, and divide yourselves into teams if necessary. Walk around the area to get a feel for the surroundings. You can also begin to set up any stationary equipment like cameras on tripods, or motion detectors. Make a note of any areas that you think may lead you to take false readings or false positive pictures. If you are indoors, take careful note of things like air vents, heaters, electrical appliances, fuse boxes and computers. Mark down the temperatures in the rooms and any EMF readings you get during this walk-through.

When everything is in place and you're ready to begin, log in your start time, weather conditions and any other relevant information. By the way, if you're supposed to be doing an outdoor ghost hunt and it's raining, snowing or foggy, reschedule it. You cannot conduct a proper investigation under these conditions. The exception is if the original eyewitnesses reported phenomena under such conditions.

Now you can start the investigation and take lots of pictures and recordings. You can either set up stationary recorders and just let them run, or you can walk around with them. With recordings, make sure afterwards that you view or listen to the whole tape.

Every investigator or team should keep a log of events and times – everything needs to be logged, no matter how trivial. If you hiccup, log it in! It may have sounded like something else to another member of your team, and they may then report it back as an unexplained noise. Be sure to note anything unusual, especially abnormal meter and temperature readings, and strange visual sightings and sounds. Also make notes of any feelings or emotions you experience, especially any that seem odd or unexplained. You can compare notes with the rest of your team after the hunt and look for similarities in readings and feelings in certain areas or at certain times.

During the investigation, draw no conclusions. Share no ideas or opinions with the witnesses or the owners of the property until all the reports, photos and tapes have been reviewed. You need to see the evidence and correlate it before you can give an educated opinion. Once these initial vigils have been conducted, you may find that your results have highlighted areas or phenomena on which to focus more attention and equipment on a subsequent investigation.

GUIDELINES FOR TAKING PICTURES

You may have videos and tape recorders running, but cameras are still perhaps the most accessible, portable and immediate pieces of equipment for use in paranormal investigation. Your camera may provide that vital piece of evidence, but you need to ensure that you use it correctly.

- Be prepared; open your film and load your camera before entering a location, since you don't know when something might happen.
- Use at least 400-speed 35mm film; 400- and 800-speeds work the best. Black-and-white film also works well.

- If you are an experienced photographer and can get your hands on it, you may want to try infra-red film, which has also had excellent results in the past.
- Make sure you note any other lights in the area, so when you view your pictures you won't mistake a street lamp for something mysterious.
- Clean the lens of your camera regularly.
- Watch for dust or dirt being stirred up in the area you are photographing. They can cause false positive pictures.
- Remove or tie up any camera straps, which can appear on film looking like a vortex if you photograph them accidentally. Long hair also needs to be tied back for similar reasons.
- Watch for reflective surfaces and note down when they occur. The flash reflected off shiny surfaces such as windows or polished tombstones can look like an anomaly.
- Let fellow investigators know when you are taking a photo so you don't blind each other (we tend to shout 'Flash!').
- In cold weather or after consuming a hot drink, be conscious of your breath and don't photograph it – it'll look like ectoplasm mist. If you think you may have done so, log that picture number so you can discard it when you develop the pictures.
- Take pictures anywhere and everywhere. If you feel something, or someone else does, take a picture. If you think you saw something, take a picture. Take

photos whenever you get a positive reading on any piece of equipment. If you think you may have a false positive, log the picture number so you can exclude that photo from the batch when they are developed.

• You may only get one or two interesting pictures for every hundred you take. Don't get discouraged! We've been at sites where we didn't get any interesting photos at all, and others where the results were much more promising.

WORKING WITH PSYCHICS AND MEDIUMS

In general, psychics are people with skills of telepathy and ESP who believe they can sense or pick up information from their environment and from other people. Sometimes, but not always, this information may come from another realm. Mediums, on the other hand, believe that they can communicate with the spirits of the dead. Many mediums are also psychic, but not all psychics are mediums.

Some paranormal investigators never work with psychics or mediums and never use techniques such as dowsing rods, ouija boards or séances. They argue that, from a scientific viewpoint, the validity of these methods can be questioned. Some investigators believe that evil spirits can be drawn to these types of activities. Others, and this includes us, prefer to explore and utilise all the options and keep an open mind. We have found that involving psychics in an investigation can be incredibly helpful.

If you are open-minded to a psychic's impressions, and ask them lots of questions about what they are sensing, and whether what they're getting is correct or misinterpreted, then they can be good to work with. They can in some cases pick up a great deal of useful information, as well as offering an interesting insight into mediumship processes.

The downside of working with psychics is that all too often they are convinced that they're right even if their perceptions are in direct contradiction to what the witnesses have perceived. They tend to have their set beliefs about ghosts, and nothing will persuade them to consider that alternative explanations may be possible. They also sometimes have trouble shifting their focus from the symbolic to the literal, which means that you could end up with a lot of interesting but ultimately vague information that you don't know what to do with.

The upside of working with good, open-minded psychics is that they have trained themselves to focus on the paranormal in a way few of the people involved in the investigation can. You can use their intuitive hunches to 'detect' more of what may be going on in a case. But remember that no psychic is one hundred per cent accurate in all cases, and a really good psychic is a rare find.

The best psychics and mediums we have worked with

are confident without being egotistical, and have good people skills and a good sense of humour, especially about themselves and what they do. We have to consider how useful the information they provide is, how open they are to having their perceptions questioned and, last but by no means least, whether or not they have a good track record, free of misperception and fraud.

Finally, don't underestimate the importance of your own perceptions. You may or may not be psychic, but all the equipment and all the séances in the world will not help if you neglect to develop your own intuition. Over the years we have learned to pay more and more attention to our own perceptions while on investigations. We have not yet seen an apparition or haunting, but we have certainly felt, heard, smelled and sensed things we simply can't explain.

WHAT IF I GET SCARED?

Paranormal phenomena can range from subtle things like knocks and cold draughts all the way up to the furniture being thrown about and full-blown apparitions. The chances are that dramatic things like this won't happen during your investigation, but you can never know that for sure.

Fear is the first reaction when something strange happens and it is a natural, normal human expression. The key is to keep your fear from turning into panic, and to try to concentrate on verifying whatever it is that you are seeing, hearing or sensing by taking notes. Even though you may be recording on a video recorder or tape machine, it's still a good idea to take written notes of your feelings too.

There have been many cases when paranormal investigators have run in fear from a location. There is no way of knowing how you will react in a situation until you are in it. We've lost count of the number of times we have felt the hairs rise on the backs of our necks, and on occasion we have halted an investigation prematurely because of some element of discomfort we could not explain but could not get past either. You've probably heard people say things like 'Ghosts can't harm you, they're dead' or 'There's nothing to be afraid of', but, however sceptical you think you are going in, you must be prepared to find yourself affected by the energy or atmosphere of a location in a way you might never have anticipated.

If you do feel afraid, try to stay calm so that your fear does not spread to the rest of the team and endanger the investigation. If you do panic, ask someone to take you home, and in the meantime separate yourself from the group and the investigation.

WHAT ARE THE SIGNS OF A HAUNTING?

We get asked this question a lot. There are many signs. Below is a list of some perceptual systems; in other words things you experience with your five senses as opposed to measurements taken with an EMF meter or IR thermometer.

Visual: Apparitions, hazes or mists, orbs. Shadows and shapes, often seen out of the corner of the eye, but sometimes seen in the centre of the vision. Seeing a person and thinking it's someone you know, only to then find out that they were somewhere else entirely at the time.

Audio: Names whispered or spoken out loud when no one is around, often mistaken for the voice of a friend or family member. A voice or voices heard where no one is present, which may be intelligible or unintelligible. Children's laughter, babies' cries, animal sounds, footsteps when no one is around, and sounds of items being moved or broken, although you subsequently find everything in its proper place and intact. There may also be the sounds of musical instruments, radios, records or televisions playing when they are not.

Smell: Many people think that different smells represent different spirits, while others believe that spirits can emit a smell that was commonly associated with them in life, for example cigarette smoke or a favourite perfume.

Tactile: Cold spots with no explanation – some say the ghost is absorbing heat energy. Hot spots with no explanation – the ghost is expelling heat energy.

Textures: You may feel skin (usually damp) in the form of a hand grabbing you, or fur, as in something like an animal rubbing or brushing against your bare leg.

Kinetic: We use this term to refer to those experiences where the activity involves a more obvious change to the physical world: some sort of movement. They can and do run the gamut of human possibility, but here is a short list:

- Items are moved or thrown across the room or slid across a surface, sometimes right off that surface.
- Items are hidden or 'lost'. About fifty per cent of the time these items will turn up some time later in very bizarre locations. For example a watch you wore yesterday and took off for the night turns up in a cupboard that has been locked for the past year. An appearing object is known as an 'apport', a disappearing object as an 'asport'.
- Mechanical equipment or fixtures activated without anyone being near them: toilets flushing, sinks and showers turning on and off, light switches flipping themselves on (see also *Electrical*, below), drawers and doors opening and closing, locks engaging or disengaging.

Electrical: Some believe that almost any electrical appliance can be affected by a spirit. For example, the TV/radio/stereo turns on and off without living influence. Fans and lights turn on and off without the switch being flipped. Perfectly healthy appliances short out or explode. Remotely operated toys, like radio-controlled cars, operate on their own.

This is by no means a comprehensive list, more a generalised group of commonly reported experiences. Most of them have been experienced by someone in our team.

So there you have the basics of paranormal investigation. Perhaps the most important piece of advice we can give you if you want to have a go yourself is: be as sceptical as possible. Always look for natural or manmade causes for any phenomenon. Remember that being 'sceptical' doesn't mean having a closed mind – in fact it means keeping an open mind about all the possible explanations, including the paranormal. Never go into an investigation with pre-drawn conclusions.

Now read on for our experiences when we carried out our investigations – at home and abroad.

PART ONE:

At Home

1

Dartford Library

When eyewitness accounts reached us about spooky goings-on at Dartford Library in Kent, we were immediately intrigued. We had never carried out an investigation in a library before, and don't know of any high-profile library cases in the UK, so we jumped at the chance to carry out this first-time investigation. It's also a personal dream come true for Ciarán, who, since being enthralled all those years ago by the movie *Ghostbusters*, has trodden a career path not dissimilar from the parapsychologists who, in one of the most famous scenes, investigate a haunting in the New York Public Library.

THE PHENOMENON OF HAUNTED LIBRARIES

Our first step after getting the chance to investigate Dartford Library was to carry out some research into other libraries with comparable histories. In the UK, with the exception of some rumours of paranormal activity in a library on the Isle of Wight – which didn't come as a surprise to us as many thousands of ghosts are alleged to haunt that island – we didn't come up with anything. Across the pond in the United States, though, we found some intriguing ghost tales among the bookshelves.

Perhaps the most famous story is that of the Snohomish Library in Washington state, which is believed to be haunted by the ghost of a female librarian, said to be one Catherine McMurchy who worked there between 1923 and 1939. The frequency of reported sightings was enough that updatable webcams were installed, to allow internet surfers to become armchair ghost-hunters and report their supernatural sightings. Before you turn to your computer and type 'Snohomish' into a search engine, though, you should know that the library has now been relocated to a new facility and, sadly, the webcams removed.

Another library in the USA that is reputedly haunted is Poseyville Carnegie Public Library in Indiana. Ever since its renovation in 1975, staff have repeatedly reported electrical disturbances, an apparition of a woman in period costume and a general sense of presence, which is sometimes so strong that some staff make a point of saying good-night to the seemingly empty library as they leave for the evening. Intriguingly, as you'll see below, some of the phenomena mentioned in the Poseyville case echo those allegedly experienced at Dartford Library.

THE CASE OF DARTFORD LIBRARY

In November 2006 we headed down to Kent, accompanied by two cameramen to record the investigation and the medium David Wells. Most of the time we prefer to work as a twosome, but in this instance we felt that the case was so unusual and the eyewitness accounts from staff members and reliable witnesses, some of whom had previously had very little interest or belief in the paranormal, so compelling that we should give ourselves the best possible chance of carrying out an extra-thorough investigation. Having someone else involved would provide an extra set of senses and be good insurance against any potential loss of objectivity. Also, leaving the recording of the experience to others would free up our concentration and allow us to maximise our skills of observation

So what has been going on at Dartford Library to merit our interest? According to recent reports from staff members and visitors, there have been several glimpses of the apparition of a woman, a phenomenon that recalls the Poseyville Library case. The exact reported details of the woman are inconsistent; in some she is described as childlike, while in others she is elderly. However, there is one detail that is consistent throughout all the reports; the apparition is always seen holding a book tightly to her chest.

Unexplained noises and creaks have also been

reported, as have several occurrences of books being discovered in locations where they didn't belong, or even particular books falling off their shelves just as a staff member entered the library in search of them. This intriguing phenomenon is, in fact, quite well known.

Library Angels

The writer Dame Rebecca West had been carrying out research in her local library all day, spending much of her time searching in vain for one particular page in one particular book. Eventually, in frustration she went to complain to a library assistant. The page she needed, she told the assistant, was somewhere here, but it could be in any one of the rows and rows of huge reference books. To demonstrate to the assistant the size of the books and of her task, Dame Rebecca made an arbitrary choice and pulled one off the shelf, then flipped it open. It fell open at exactly the page that she had been looking for.

Dame Rebecca West tells this story in a letter of 1972 to Arthur Koestler (who established a Chair of Parapsychology at the University of Edinburgh). In his book *The Challenge of Chance*, Koestler gives many other examples of this phenomenon, which he calls 'Library Angels'. A Library Angel is thought to be the explanation for situations like the one experienced by Dame Rebecca and witnessed by the assistant; those fortuitous moments in the search for books, quotations or even single words. Essentially, a Library Angel is the spiritual version of the perfect Research Assistant!

Despite the Library Angels, the unexplained groans and tapping noises, and the sightings of the ghostly librarian, what seemed to freak out Dartford staff members the most and leave the strongest impression was actually the inexplicable atmosphere of menace that many people have reported feeling in the library. This sensation seems to be at its strongest in the oldest part of the building, the upstairs reference section. Obviously this was one area we would have to pay particular attention to when we started our investigation.

On the way down to Kent we did some of our own research on the history of Dartford Library to see if it would offer us any clues or leads to the alleged paranormal activity going on there. We discovered that it was built between 1914 and 1915, right in the midst of the disruption and chaos of the First World War, making it nearly ninety-five years old. The library seems to have been a great success in the community right from its opening; in 1916, over 77,000 books were issued to 2,775 borrowers. By 1933 nearly a quarter of a million books a year were being issued, incredibly by the near-heroic efforts of only four members of staff. The library proved to be so popular, in fact, that in its twentieth-birthday year, 1936, it was expanded. With so many people having come and gone through its doors ever since the First World War, it does not seem surprising to us that the library may also have attracted some spectral visitors over the years!

During the Second World War, the library played an important role in keeping the public informed and boosting morale. It even had its own team of wardens, who would climb on to the roof during an air raid to watch out for any incendiary device that might hit the building or surrounding area. After the war ended the library continued to play an important role at the heart of the community, using new ideas and techniques. Book displays, talks, visits and exhibitions to inform, educate, entertain and inspire were continued and developed.

We discovered that the library building also houses a museum, the Dartford Borough Museum, which tells the story of the town and its surrounding area from prehistoric times to the present day. The museum, which was moved to the same site as the library in the 1920s, interestingly enough has as yet attracted no reports of paranormal activity.

It was clear to us that Dartford Library had been a success story right from its beginnings. The question for us was: why, in such a positive, robust and inspiring environment, did visitors and staff members experience this often-reported sensation of a menacing and irksome presence lingering among the bookshelves?

Venturing in

We arrive at Dartford Library in the daytime. The town is bustling with lunchtime business, office workers hurriedly grabbing a quick sandwich, uninterested shoppers racing past windows whilst mothers navigate their buggies round the busy throngs. The majority of the town in the vicinity of the library reflects retail development from the last twenty years. It is full of modern shops and cafés. It is only when we're facing the front of the library, about to enter, are we suddenly transported elsewhere. Our senses have been bombarded with the chaos of the town but now we are suddenly struck by the eary calm that surrounds the entrance to the library. Small, well-kept public gardens are laid out in front and there is an immediate serenity. It is cheesy to say it but we both give each other a nervous look that says 'this is the calm before the storm'.

In addition to being transported from a racket to peacefullness, we're also taken to a different era. The contemporary shopfronts have given way to a building from decades and decades ago. If we don't turn and look to our left we could easily be standing in the Dartford of the 1950s or even earlier. For a fleeting moment, as we push open the heavy wooden doors and enter the library, we do feel as though we have walked through a time warp. We immediately correct ourselves and start to feel incredibly excited about the forthcoming investigation. Excited, but also now a little uneasy.

We ask the staff to turn off all the lights, and in hushed silence we enter the main section of the library. The shelving and arrangement of the interior is modern, your typical town library. Although it would not fit anyone's idea of a conventional spooky-looking place, the experience of being in a library at night is new and eerie for us both. We shine our torches from crowded bookshelf to crowded bookshelf and empty desk to empty desk. The torchlight casts shadows through the gaps, our quick glances down the aisles only making us more nervous. We move towards the centre of the library and, as we do so, we suddenly hear a loud tapping sound. All of us, including the two cameramen, hear it and stop, each of us holding our breath, to listen. The tapping continues for over a minute, then without warning the lights go on, making us all jump. Unnerved, we go to the staffroom to speak to the staff. One of the senior librarians tells us that the lights shouldn't come on like that and that even our motion in the room shouldn't have triggered them. He goes into the room to turn each of the six lights off again with a remote control.

The experience has made us feel extremely nervy, but our curiosity is stronger than our apprehension and we continue the investigation. Recalling the alleged witnessing of books being displaced or falling from their shelf as a librarian enters the library in search of them, we both try thinking hard about a particular book. Ciarán chooses Jung's *Synchronicity* and Yvette chooses Jilly Cooper's *Wicked*. Ciarán walks expectantly towards the psychology section and Yvette to the popular fiction aisle to see if their respective books fall off the shelf, but they are both firmly settled in their places.

Undeterred, we decide to go into the back office,

which is where most reported sightings of the library's lady ghost have taken place. Yvette calls out, asking if there is anybody here who lived and worked here in the past, and if we can help in any way. We listen carefully for several minutes but hear nothing, not even a recurrence of the tapping.

Yvette: *I thought graveyards at night were scary but I can honestly say that I think libraries in the dark are scarier! It's something to do with all those books waiting to be read; untold stories and adventures. It's very Harry Potter for me in here and I half-expect a book to come flying off the shelf and land in my hands. The tapping and the lights going on by themselves really freaked me out when we arrived, and now we are in the back office I can feel myself shaking even though I've got Ciarán here with me and the two cameramen. Can't explain why but I don't like it in this room. In fact I don't like being in this library at all. It's as if someone wants me to leave, just doesn't want me here. I'm really scared about going upstairs to the oldest part of the building. I'm glad we have David, our medium, with us if we need him.*

Ciarán: *Wow! I'm used to a lot of waiting and listening on an investigation before we get anything, but here, as soon as we stepped into the library and turned the lights off, we heard the tapping and then the lights switched themselves on. At first I thought that the tapping might be due to central heating, birds nesting or even rain, but when I went outside to check there were no birds on the roof and it wasn't raining. There was a full moon though! As for the lights, I suspected that it might be an electrical fault but have been told this isn't the case. Considering the lights coming on was coincident with the tapping, it could be an electrical motor that we heard, something to do with the lights' sensors that the staff haven't considered. It's all very intriguing. I'm a bit concerned about Yvette as she is even more jumpy than usual. She is telling me she doesn't like it here but so far I don't feel anything but curiosity. I'm keen to move on with the investigation.*

We are determined to give the downstairs one last attempt before moving on. We'll pay particular attention to any tapping sounds and try to find a source. We also decide that we're going to try something to get a reaction out of the ghostly librarians. In a section of the library near the back office there is a large rack full of a great variety of magazines, some of which we take out and place in a messy pattern on the floor. We leave via the room's only exit and start another vigil in the main part of the library. Yvette calls out, asking the spirits to tidy up the magazines that have been left strewn on the floor. We then walk a slow circuit around the bookshelves, willing books to come flying off their shelves. Occasionally Ciarán steps into some of the alcoves to look at temperature differences and take scans with the thermal imager.

We briefly hear the tapping again and it sounds, this time, as though it's definitely coming from above us. We both look up and realise that there's no floor directly above us, so the most likely explanation is that the tapping noise is, as Ciarán suspected, connected to a fault in the lighting system. A little disappointed, we return to the pile of magazines, hoping to find them back in their ordered arrangement on the racks. Unfortunately though, that little test hasn't produced results and we have to replace them ourselves. As we walk back through the library, a light suddenly comes on. It makes Yvette jump violently and we walk hastily back to the office to find the senior librarian again. Ciarán insists on switching off the light himself this time, and double-checks every single light before placing the remote control in his pocket so we won't have to find our way back to the office if anything else happens with the lights.

Yvette: *Trying to provoke a reaction from spirits who might haunt a place is sometimes the best way to get evidence, I find. On some previous investigations I've even become quite emotional and challenged the spirits for more. I always know my boundaries though and David often pulls on the reins, as it were, to ensure that I don't stray over to a darker side. I liked the idea of making some books or magazines untidy, and it fitted the location, it's just a shame it didn't work. These lights are unnerving me – just when I think nothing's going to happen, one goes on. Now, if they all came on at once at my command that would be something!*

Ciarán: *I find it strange being tarnished with the 'sceptic' or 'cynic' label, because I find it very difficult to wander around a location like Dartford Library and not be wishing for something to happen. Even if there turns out to be a rational explanation, that instant jolt of adrenalin as something unexpected happens is great. Let's hope a book flies across the room and lands on the floor in front of us! It was a good idea of Yvette's to try and get the ghostly librarian into tidy-up mode. Maybe we could try something similar later.*

Footsteps in the Dark

We ask David, who has been waiting in a car outside, to join us; Yvette wants his input on the phenomena we have already experienced. David's sedate presence immediately has a positive effect on Yvette, calming her down and giving her time to think about the next investigative step. In a moment of boldness she suggests heading upstairs, although she insists on being sandwiched between Ciarán, David and the cameramen.

The walk upstairs is an adventure in itself, with hidden back stairs via a storeroom, then a narrow, pitch-black corridor running between imposing shelves stacked to the ceiling with catalogue files. We walk up the final set of stairs from the catalogue room, open a creaky door at the top and walk around the creepy attic section. It is home to hundreds of reference books, files and museum exhibits. A desk that's normally busy, used for cataloguing exhibits, tonight has an empty chair as its only companion. We're conscious, however that even though we can't see anyone, spectral companions may be watching us. We shoot worried and tense glances down one of the very long passages at the side of the room, acutely aware that a face might at any moment poke out from one of the aisles off it and stare right back at us. We all notice that it feels much colder up here than downstairs and we aren't sure why, although Ciarán has a theory to do with electric fields.

David drinks in the atmosphere and almost immediately tells us that he senses a female presence. Yvette asks what her name is and he tells us it is Kathleen and that she is neither young nor old, but somehow both. He tells us that she knows we are here but her grief is preventing her from opening up to us. She is crying in the corner and clutching a book tightly to her chest. We ask David if he can see what the book is about, but he says he can't read the title and she won't tell him. What he does sense, however, is that books are very important to this lady. She is incredibly lonely, and afraid of both us and someone else.

We continue to wander around the attic, creeping along a long passage, ducking at times to avoid the low sloping ceiling. As we approach the far end of the attic, both Yvette and David suddenly turn around, saying that they hear footsteps following us. Now all the physical signs of fear are really kicking in. The hairs on the backs of their necks stand on end, they are feeling a tightness in their throats and their hearts are beating faster, pumping blood round the body. At this tense point, Ciarán yells out to take a look at something on the thermal imager. Eagerly we all peer into the lens and see what appears to be a single pair of fresh footsteps walking towards us. They have followed us along the passage, almost stalking us. We are all silent and our mouths drop open. The realisation that a phantom stalker is here in the attic freezes us to the spot. The footsteps can't be ours: there would be more than one set. Also, they look to us like male footsteps, the kind made by large, flat men's shoes. Definitely not Yvette's then; she is wearing low heels.

While we are still reeling from the sight of the footsteps, David announces that he feels a rush of sudden male energy, and that this male energy wants us to leave. We look back at the footsteps and to our surprise they have vanished. At this point, although Ciarán is excited, both Yvette and David feel shocked and uneasy. Everyone's heart is beating faster, but for entirely different reasons. Now Yvette and David are frantically scanning every shadow, every aisle, eager to find something but also dreading a sudden scare. They both feel a tightening in their chests and a hollowness in their stomachs. Yvette is convinced that something in the room wants us to leave. As we head back downstairs to appease the angry male presence, we hear a faint bang coming from upstairs. Glad to be back in the light and warmth of the reception area, we take some time to reflect on an eventful few hours.

Yvette: *I've been to places where hideous things like torture or execution have happened and not felt as scared and uneasy as I did in this library. The atmosphere of the place is heavy and odd and I definitely would not want to be here alone. You have no idea what is lurking amongst the bookshelves. According to David there is a melancholic female presence here and although I didn't see or hear anything I think I did pick up on her sadness. It wasn't until we had finished the investigation and I sat down with a hot cup of tea and the lights were on that my mood shifted and I stopped feeling so low. I think if I stayed or worked upstairs for any length of time I would end up feeling very depressed. Is that me being empathic towards the sad woman up there? I have no idea who that lady was but she was unhappy for sure, and her sadness may have been to do with the rush of violent male energy David also picked up on. I really wish I could help her but I don't know how. I may well ask David to try again at a later date to communicate with her. I won't go with him though, since I don't want to experience again what I have tonight. Hand on heart, Dartford Library is one of the most unusual haunted places I've ever encountered.*

Downstairs, in the main part of the library, it wasn't so bad, not threatening in any way, but as soon as we went upstairs I was absolutely terrified. The menacing nature of that attic didn't surprise me as librarians have reported the same thing. Maybe there was an elderly gentleman who loved working there so much he feels it is his property and he wants everyone to leave. For such an angry spirit to be roaming around upstairs there must be a reason. Everything else that happened was totally unexpected. Then again that's why I love this job; my expectations are constantly being challenged. Nothing is predictable, certainly not the fact that a library at night would end up being more terrifying to me than any haunted dungeon!

Ciarán: *Although there is no proof, one theory about haunted locations is that they can somehow 'record' intense emotions that have been experienced in them. This is sometimes called a 'residual haunting'. We'll discuss this theory in more detail in Part Two when we relive our visit to the Château du Pays Lauragais, but in brief, the theory suggests that some locations act as giant storage tapes, saving up and memorising the impressions of sights and sounds from the past. Then, as the years go by, these impressions spontaneously appear again as if a film projector has started to run. In the case of Dartford Library it's possible that the images witnessed by others may have been created by events or actions that were repeated over and over again, and the constant repetition has caused an impression on the atmosphere that can be picked up by allegedly highly sensitive people like David. In Dartford Library, over its long history the stairs and reference section have been extensively used by librarians and members of the public. I'm not one hundred per cent convinced by the theory though, especially in a location like this where I can't really imagine there would be a lot of intense emotion. That would be much more understandable in a location like a castle or a battlefield.*

Bit of physics for you now – electric field readings in the attic, measured in volts/metre, revealed almost a wave pattern moving from the front of the area to the back at head height. The readings were set at ELF, meaning it was detecting electrosmog with very low frequencies – below 500Hz. The readings I was getting could point to a possible explanation for the oppressive, even cold and menacing feeling staff get there.

It could be argued that David's presence upstairs acted as some kind of catalyst. The difficulty is that we never spent time in the attic area without David to see if anything happened then – in other words we didn't have a 'control condition' as you would in most experiments. I know that he wasn't provided with any information in advance about the paranormal activity reported at the library, so it was amazing that he 'saw' the librarian holding a book, although a sceptic such as myself might argue that it's hardly surprising to come up with a librarian 'spirit' in a library! He also sensed a malevolent male energy that didn't want us in the building. I was intrigued rather than scared by the investigation, but I know Yvette and David very well and over the years that I've worked with them both I don't recall seeing either so anxious or eager to leave.

Conclusion

We didn't pick up evidence tying into all of the previous eyewitness testimonies from the library. We do have, however, so many things about this case to reflect on in the coming months. The tapping and the lights going on were surprising enough, but they paled into insignificance next to the footsteps that appeared on our thermal imager. After the investigation we double-checked our equipment and the room with the lights on, but we're convinced there were no underfloor sources of heat in the room to generate the footsteps we saw. The only natural explanation is that the footsteps belonged to one of us, but if they did, then why weren't there three sets of footsteps? Was it something to do with the soles of our shoes? Perhaps one set had less insulation than another? Perhaps one of us had warmer feet or circulated more heat?

This is all speculation, however, and it leaves the question of where they could have come from if they didn't belong to one of us. Until we're in a position to test all possibilities, it wouldn't be scientific of us not to include paranormal activity as one possible explanation.

2

Allerton Tower

'One autumnal afternoon several years ago, whilst writing
and researching a volume of *Haunted Liverpool*, I decided
to take a much-needed break, having been hunched over
my computer for most of the day. I set off for a walk
which took me down Menlove Avenue, past Calderstone's
Park and into another, almost deserted park, where I
dwelt upon the Gothic splendour of Allerton Tower's ruins.
I strolled through the vestiges of the palatial home which I
knew had once belonged to the illustrious Earle family; the
magnificent remains of a legendary grandiose residence,
now sadly left to the mercy of the English weather, idiotic
vandals and mindless graffiti 'artists'. As I lingered near
the shell of an outbuilding on the long-lost, seventy-eight
acre estate of Allerton Tower, something just glimpsed out
the corner of my eye flitted past me. I half-turned reflex-
ively, but the flitting 'thing' had vanished, leaving a sweet
scent in its wake. I immediately wondered if the fabled
Grey Lady of the ruins had just brushed past me. I

certainly had not imagined that entity and it had not been a trick of the light. Some ghosts are quite timid, and manifest themselves so briefly that they come and go in the twinkling of an eye. The Grey Lady of the ruins has been seen by numerous witnesses over the years, and several years ago I was told the tragic story which lay behind the haunting of Allerton Tower . . .'

EYEWITNESS ACCOUNT IN *HAUNTED LIVERPOOL 1* BY TOM SLEMEN, 2006.

THE CASE OF ALLERTON TOWER

Allerton Tower manor house is an abandoned ruin located in Allerton Towers public park in Liverpool. The house dates back to the eleventh century so, not surprisingly, it has changed hands many times. In the eighteenth and nineteenth centuries it belonged to the Hartley family, who were railway magnates, but after they left no one else could afford to take on the upkeep and so the house was left to rot. Ancient ruins often have ghost stories associated with them but, as you'll see from the story below, surely few can be as compelling and as tragic as the haunted history of Allerton Tower.

In the 1850s, the very wealthy Sir Hardman Earle, influential director of the Liverpool–Manchester Railway, lived at Allerton Tower with his large family, which included three sons: Thomas, Arthur and William. In spite of Hardman Earle's standing there were persistent rumours about the dishonest and corrupt ways in which he may have gained his fortune.

These whispers of intrigue add a dark backdrop to an already terrible tragedy.

One night the brothers visited a local tavern, where they enjoyed the company of three girls. By the end of the night William, at seventeen the youngest of the three, had lost his virginity and was recklessly declaring his love for a pretty young Irish girl called Mary. She was not of a social class and background considered suitable for a son of Hardman Earle, though, and so William's two brothers wrestled him away from the girl and, on their walk home, tried to stamp out his talk of love.

Despite his brothers' warnings, William seized every opportunity to sneak off and meet his beloved Mary. The two became inseparable and planned to elope together. It wasn't long before Sir Hardman Earle came to hear about the secret meetings, and his reaction was to give William a severe beating and lock him in his room. The eldest brother, Thomas, also visited Mary and warned her to stay away from William. On hearing this, Mary began to cry bitterly and told Thomas she was pregnant with William's child. Thomas knew that if word got out about the pregnancy it would create a shameful family scandal. To make matters worse, the sobbing girl admitted that she had already told her Uncle Desmond.

Thomas returned to Allerton Tower and told his brother Arthur the story. They came to the conclusion that they could not risk Mary's uncle trying to blackmail them with this scandalous information, and that the only solution was to kill both Mary and Desmond. A few days later, appropriately on a stormy night, Thomas lured Mary to a secluded wood. There she was ambushed and brutally bludgeoned to death by both brothers.

Arthur was full of regret when he fully realised what he had done to the pregnant girl, but Thomas, who it seems had inherited a greater measure of his father's ruthlessness, slapped him and told him this was no time for regrets and faint-heartedness, and that they had had no alternative. The brothers carried the girl's limp and mangled body across a field and dropped her into the depths of an old well at the far end. The following night her uncle Desmond, was killed by a horse whose rider was a man dressed in a long black cloak with a lowered hat-brim covering most of his face.

Mary's body was discovered in the well and the locals immediately suspected foul play. The death of her uncle in the same week also aroused their suspicions and a local Romany was asked to use dowsing to divine the murderer. He took the villagers directly to Allerton Tower. Sir Hardman Earle managed to scatter the villagers by confronting them with a loaded shotgun. For the present at least, the Earle brothers had got away with their crime.

Several weeks later, however, the brothers did reap the consequence of their actions; the apparition of a pale-faced girl with bedraggled, dripping hair and soaking-wet clothes appeared to both of them in their bedrooms. Her appearance, covered in terrible wounds, emanating immeasurable sadness and pointing an accusing finger, terrified them and left them both emotional wrecks, doomed never to enjoy a peaceful night's sleep again. Mary also sought retribution on their father, appearing at his deathbed. In a final manifestation she apparently made herself visible to her young lover William Earle, this time looking loving and peaceful, on the eve of his death in 1885.

Since then, the ghost of a pale and beautiful pregnant lady has been seen on numerous occasions, treading forlornly and moaning softly among the ruins of the tower. She has come to be known as the Grey Lady of Allerton Tower.

Grey Ladies

'Grey Lady' is the term used to describe the ghost of a woman who, like Mary at Allerton Tower, is said to have died violently for the sake of love or through the heartless actions of a family member or loved one. Grey Ladies have been reported all over the world but many incidents and sightings are associated with ruins and events dating from around Tudor times. This makes a great deal of sense considering that during this period the destruction of abbeys and monasteries in England caused the death of many nuns, who at the time dressed in grey. The most well-known Grey Ladies are those reported to haunt Newstead Abbey, Rufford Old Hall, Denbigh Castle, Glamis Castle, and Holy Trinity Church in Micklegate, York.

We have been involved in a Grey Lady case ourselves; we were part of a televised investigation of Chambercombe Manor in Ilfracombe, North Devon, which has reportedly been haunted by a Grey Lady since the seventeenth century. Legend has it that the leaseholder of the manor house, William Oatway, deliberately lured a ship ashore on a stormy night so it would crash on the rocks and he could plunder it. A female survivor was washed ashore, her face so badly beaten that she was unrecognisable. William carried her to the manor house, where he and his wife tried desperately to save her life, but her injuries proved too serious and later that night she died without regaining consciousness.

As William and his wife searched her body for some clue to her identity, they found a money belt strapped around her waist. Opening it, William discovered that it contained enough gold coins and jewels to enable him to achieve his most cherished ambition – he would be able to buy Chambercombe Manor. The temptation proved too great, and with a shaking hand William reached out and relieved the dead woman of her valuables.

The next morning, a shipping agent came by to enquire if they had any knowledge of a woman passenger who was missing off a wrecked ship. Realising that if he admitted to having found the woman he would probably be forced to return the valuables, William denied all knowledge of her. As the agent was leaving he asked William to keep an eye on the coastline in case the body of the woman,

Mrs Katherine Wallace, should be washed up. Katherine Wallace was the married name of William's daughter, who had recently moved to live in Dublin with her Irish husband. Grief-stricken, frightened and ashamed, William walled his daughter's body up in a secret chamber. He and his wife then swiftly departed Chambercombe Manor, never to return.

A century or so later the chamber was discovered and Katherine's bones were removed and buried in a pauper's grave. Many say that her ghost still lingers in the house where she grew up with William Oatway, her father – and murderer.

Our investigation begins

It's the middle of the night and we are standing just outside the entrance to Allerton Towers Park in Liverpool. The park is a public one, with vast open green spaces and a woodland area. It is next to Allerton Golf Course and forms part of a series of beautiful green expanses in the Allerton and Woolton area of Liverpool. Thankfully the park is open twenty-four hours a day, so we are free to conduct a late-night investigation. We've got Yvette's husband Karl and another experienced cameraman with us, plus Andy, a local psychologist friend of Ciarán's. For safety reasons, it makes sense to have a larger group in this sort of location at night. We must reiterate here that with any investigation of a public location, it is essential to get permission or make the relevant authorities aware of what you're doing. Ciarán had already been in touch with the local council and the park rangers to make them aware of our intentions. They were very helpful and wished us good luck, but made it clear that they wouldn't be joining us on our hunt for ghosts!

Of our group, Ciarán knows about the background and haunting associated with Allerton Tower but the rest of the group are in the dark, figuratively as well as literally! Ciarán has decided not to tell the others anything about the haunting, in order to keep the investigation as impartial as possible.

We haven't a plan and are simply going to explore the park and manor to see if we can discover or experience anything. It's guerrilla ghost-hunting at its best, and at this stage we all agree that we feel excited rather than frightened. If anything we are more scared of the living jumping out at us than the dead, because there could easily be tramps or drunks loitering here.

With our cameras rolling, we leave the main road behind us and enter the park. It's a mass of trees, shadows and darkness. As soon as we are inside, Ciarán tells us that our investigation has officially begun and that we need to immediately be on our guard, as eyewitnesses have reported phenomena not just in the ruins of Allerton Tower but also in the park grounds.

Ciarán: *This investigation is environmentally very different to anywhere we have investigated before simply because of the scale. There have been various ghost sightings, not only near the manor but also all round the park. No harm has actually come to anyone who has wandered here at night but there are stories of dark intrigue associated with at least one of the hauntings.*

Yvette: *I'm really not frightened at all at the moment but this may be to do with the fact that I'm here with four guys! I don't know how I'd feel if I was on my own. It's also not as dark as I thought it might be. I think my eyes are getting used to it – I can see just ahead of me. I like the idea of us simply wandering and exploring a location and it's a real treat to be investigating such a large area outside as most of the time we are confined to rooms or buildings. At the same time I'm a little nervous because Ciarán seems excited by our investigation, and when he's excited it normally means it'll be a scary one!*

We make our way into the centre of the park and approach Allerton Tower. We shine our torches to get a better look and see a covered walkway that, although it is covered in striking foliage, seems run-down and dilapidated. Ciarán tells us that although people have seen things in the surrounding park, the focus of the reported paranormal activity has mainly been in or near the ruins of the tower. This walkway is all that's left of Allerton Tower's orangery, a sort of extravagant greenhouse popular in those days, which were often built as a display of wealth.

Ciarán: *This is an incredible sight. From the outside it looks impressive, a grandiose hint of what was there in the past. Actually in the orangery itself, looking along its length, you can see how run-down it is, surrounded by broken plaster and graffiti. It's also a little spooky-looking along this walkway, not being able to see what's at the far end. I'm going to set up a locked-off camera at this point before we go further into the grounds. I'm doing this because there have been reports of apparitions in this area and I want to make sure we don't miss anything. Andy is also going to stay here and keep an eye on the camera and surroundings.*

Yvette: *I'm feeling a bit sad at this point as we stand outside the ruins of Allerton Tower. Even in the dark I can see that it was once a beautiful place, but it has been destroyed by time, weather and vandalism. It makes me angry that such a lovely building should have been left to rot. It's a shame because with all the graffiti on the walls and the litter on the floor it looks seedy, but it clearly wasn't always like this. Once it must have been magnificent. I'm very conscious that it is getting darker and as I peek my head round and look down the walkway greeting us I get a little apprehensive.*

We tentatively walk the full length of the covered walkway and come to an area of overgrown trees and bushes. We have to duck and weave our way through, but beyond this thicket we discover a derelict red-brick building with a series of arches. As we venture closer we see litter, grime, dust and dirt everywhere and, quite disturbingly, a burned and discarded woman's coat. The mood has changed for us all as we scramble over the rubble and enter the building. We all feel very apprehensive. We edge through a broken and creaking door into a large room that may once have been a living room. There are remnants of a brick fireplace and the windows have been bricked up, making us feel a bit claustrophobic. Here too there is litter, junk and graffiti everywhere. And the place stinks!

Yvette starts to call out in the hope that she might make contact with a lingering presence. She asks if there are any spirit beings here who wish to make their presence felt, and asks them to tap twice for yes and once for no. Yvette is convinced that she feels two taps under her right foot. She asks for two taps if the spirit is male and one if it is female, and almost immediately says she feels two taps again. Yvette is freaked out but Ciarán, Stuart and Karl didn't hear or feel anything. Ciarán tells Yvette that it was probably rats, or perhaps water dripping somewhere. He also wonders if the brooding, run-down atmosphere of the place is heightening Yvette's responses. He reminds us that given the abandoned look and feel of the place, all of us, himself included, are in danger of being prone to suggestion.

Suggestion

If you are told a place is haunted, that people who have lived there saw and felt things, you are more likely to have similar experiences than if you had been told nothing. This psychological process is called suggestion and has been known about for some time. It has a connection with two more psychological phenomena, the placebo effect and hypnosis.

Imagine you are part of a medical study looking into a new cure for the common cold. You would be given either the cure or a placebo (a 'pretend' cure, which may be just water or a sugar pill), without being told which one you were receiving. The placebo effect is the body reacting to the placebo as if it were the real thing. Scientists are aware that some people receiving the placebo may actually spontaneously recover from their colds. It is almost as though your body has been fooled into thinking that it is receiving the cure. The effect relies on the individual responding to the suggestion that they are receiving the actual cure.

In hypnosis, too, the power of suggestion is key; a person under hypnosis is in such a different and receptive state of mind that they can be fooled by a simple suggestion into thinking and acting as if they have a weightless arm or that they are hungry, or even, as in some stage-hypnosis acts, that they are a famous musician or a stripper.

Take this power of suggestion and apply it to haunting

investigations, and the effect can be amazing. In a study back in 2000 that Ciarán co-authored with a university team from Hertfordshire and Edinburgh, he looked at exactly this idea. Members of the public who were visiting Hampton Court Palace were told that the Haunted Gallery had been the focus of recent paranormal activity, split into two groups and asked to walk around either that gallery or the Georgian Rooms and report back any unusual, potentially paranormal, experiences. At least, that is what happened half the time. The rest of the time the situation was reversed. The public were told that it was the Georgian Rooms that had recently seen paranormal goings-on. What happened? Those people who said they were believers in the paranormal reported significantly more experiences in whichever area of the palace they had been told was haunted. The extra-ordinary power of existing belief in the paranormal combined with a bit of suggestion!

There's no doubt that suggestion, or suggestibility, plays a significant role in investigating 'haunted' locations. It also plays a part when there are groups of people investigating; this is the phenomenon of collective behaviour, which is also related to the social-psychology concept of group conformity. This means that in a group setting, people become highly suggestible to each other's restlessness or fear; if one says they sense something unusual or suspicious, others are likely to have – or believe they're having – similar experiences.

Imagine all this going on in a location that is reportedly haunted! It seems fairly likely under these circumstances that one person's fear or belief will infect another. Could this be what is happening to us here at Allerton? It's certainly possible.

Yvette tells Ciarán that she is all too aware of the power of suggestion in a place like this but she is still feeling shaky. We decide to leave the living room and go back outside to calm her nerves. On our way out Yvette's torch goes out, which panics her even more, because prior to every investigation we always make sure our torches are fitted with new batteries; there is no way Yvette's battery should have run out this early. We try to keep a sense of perspective as Ciarán tells us that it is highly likely that the battery or connection was faulty. We regroup with Andy, who has nothing to report, and venture further.

Just like Sleepy Hollow

We walk around the park some more, venturing through various brambly arches and among hidden wooded areas before heading back into the main park. The groomed paths and picturesque flowerbeds of this main space contrast starkly with the dark, shadowy wooded areas, but even walking here the shadows of the surrounding trees seem to have a menacing quality about them. We see a small building with the lights on. It's an extension to the red-brick building we encountered earlier on. Ciarán goes inside to investigate, emerging to report that the man he found inside is part of a local youth-education group that specialises in outdoor education in the area. We won't be able to investigate this particular building as it is all locked up and only open to the youth trust. We can't help wondering what the man is doing here so late at night, though. Ciarán jokingly suggests that perhaps he is a ghost!

We stay within the tower's grounds and explore some more in the woods on the other side of the red-brick building. Yvette lightens the mood by mentioning the film *Sleepy Hollow* and we all agree that there is that kind of Gothic feel here. There's a moment of shock as a bird swoops down on us. Once we have recovered our composure and had a good laugh about how easily startled we are, Yvette decides to call out again to try to persuade any spirits that might be present to communicate. Although there is no response, we are feeling a little excited now as we've discovered what looks like a tunnel. It's very dark and we have to duck to avoid the low stone ceiling. At the end we come to a round room without a ceiling. It looks as though it may once have been a well of some kind, now filled in. Gratefully we stand up straight, but now we're a little nervous as the only exit is back through the tunnel. Yvette continues to call out, and while she is doing so we hear a muffled bang coming from what sounds like the inside of the tunnel. It makes us all freeze momentarily, but then Yvette can't stand the suspense any more and breaks it by asking Ciarán to tell us what ghosts have been seen here.

Ciarán tells us that he will give us the details, but not before he has conducted a short experiment. First he asks if Yvette thinks the tapping she heard earlier and the bang she has just heard is a spirit. She says firmly that the answer is yes. Ciarán then surprises everyone by holding his hands over Yvette's eyes and asking her to tell us what she senses about the spirit. Yvette says she feels that the spirit is a man in his mid-thirties with curly dark hair and a pale complexion. Ciarán pushes her further, asking if she has any feelings about this man's occupation, the dates of his life, or any emotions she's picking up on. Yvette says she thinks he may have been a clergyman. She's not sure about this, but she is sure that he is very angry, aggressive and evil, and wants us to leave. When Ciarán asks Yvette what time period the spirit belongs to, she replies that he lived in the 1800s, that his name may have been John, and that he had two brothers.

Ciarán: *I've just asked Yvette to work blind and focus on what's in her mind. It was really interesting for me because I know the history of the place, whereas she hasn't a clue. It's difficult to assess accuracy in this sort of situation, but that's not why I did it. Some of what she came up with seemed to relate to the history but some didn't – the 'clergyman' idea and the name John, for instance. It's an interesting exercise in 'population stereotyping'. By that what I mean is; if I had done the same thing with a different person, would they have come up with the same information as Yvette simply because of what they had seen elsewhere in the park? Is it a standard story that anyone could and would have come up with, or is there something else at work? For example, guesswork could possibly have led Yvette to come up with three brothers, but it does seem like quite a coincidence!*

Yvette: *I hate it when Ciarán puts me on the spot like that to see what my mind comes up with – I'm not a psychic or a medium! Then again, it seems to have been a worthwhile exercise because he's telling me that I got some of the details right. I'm feeling quite pleased with myself. But there's something else that is suddenly making me uneasy. I'm feeling a pressure on my upper back as if someone is trying to push me away. I don't like anyone, living or dead, to push me around and it's making me angry, or perhaps I'm picking up on the negative energy in this place. I'm going to ask the guys to take me back to the living room where I heard the taps. But before we go back I want Ciarán to tell us all he knows about this place.*

Now that we have soaked up the atmosphere of Allerton Tower we all feel ready to hear about the history of the place, and Ciarán obliges. After he has finished telling us the tragic story of Mary and William we all stand for a while, deep in thought. We are mesmerised by the tale, and it's difficult for us not to feel emotional about Mary and William, and saddened and angered by the story of her violent murder.

Yvette is eager to see if any spirits will respond to her now that she knows the story of Allerton Tower. We head back inside the ruin, to the room where Yvette heard the tapping earlier. She starts to call out again and our hearts skip a beat when we all hear a loud creak. Yvette asks for two creaks if there is any spirit person present, and almost immediately we hear two creaks. She wants to know if the creaking is caused by a man and asks for two creaks for yes and one for no. Incredibly, we hear two creaks. Yvette then asks if the noise is being caused by one of the Hardman Earle brothers, and we can hardly contain our excitement when we hear two creaks again.

As we know all about the brothers and their terrible actions now, we feel a bit freaked out, so Ciarán suggests that we break the tension by shuffling about and changing position, as we have been standing still listening intently for quite a while. After we have moved around Ciarán points out that he was also conducting a little test to see if our movement caused any creaking; it didn't but, true to form, he still hasn't discounted the possibility that it is us making the noises. We stand still again but first each of us briefly shifts our weight to double-check that it is not one of us causing the noise. We don't hear anything. This time Ciarán decides to call out, and he does so in a much more aggressive way than Yvette. He asks if the gypsies and locals knew about the murder, and in response we hear very loud creaking and a bang coming from outside the room. Even though we all feel very nervous Ciarán calls out again, but this time we hear nothing; absolute silence descends. We wait silently and patiently for another half an hour, but hear nothing. We are all like statues, barely daring even to breathe. Realising that the tension has made us all feel exhausted and that our energy is spent, we reluctantly decide to call it a night.

Conclusion

Yvette: *Once again Ciarán has chosen a really fascinating and unique place for us. I have no idea how he finds them! I particularly loved this investigation as the love story it centred round featured individuals called William and Mary, the names of my children. Allerton Tower was a frightening place, whether we were in and around the ruins or out in the woods. That surprises me, since much of the time we were outside, so I didn't feel hemmed in, and I had four guys around to calm my nerves. The story of the place gave me a lump in my throat. In fact the whole experience was a bit of an emotional roller coaster. I was full of excitement at the beginning, when we came into the park, then deep sorrow when I saw the walkway for the first time, then absolute fear when in the derelict living room, then excitement and anger in the tunnel while being practically blindfolded, then sadness when I heard the story of the tower, then finally fear. Phew! I wish I could say that the presence I felt was benevolent and female and was the Grey Lady that everyone talks about, but it was definitely male, and very aggressive. Curiously, it seems that I didn't tune into Mary, which is what you might have expected, but instead tuned in to one of her murderers. It seems that in death as well as in life, his energy is the more powerful.*

Ciarán: *Allerton Tower is derelict, decrepit and, at night, creepy. With a location like that it's hard not to let your imagination run wild, so I'm not sure how to interpret tonight's result. I'm really glad we came here, though, not just because of the sinister history of the place, but also because in my mind there's a possibility, and once again I stress the word 'possibility', that we may be dealing with a genuine haunted location. The fact that there are testimonies from people who say they've seen the Grey Lady figure, even though the tower's background and history is not common knowledge, is intriguing. In addition I enjoyed the test with Yvette and I think she did too. Despite this I'm still sceptical about whether any of the events experienced tonight were paranormal. As with any ghost investigation, it's very difficult to spontaneously control an area, to make sure that at any instant there is no other possible explanation for any experienced phenomenon. For that reason, taps and bangs that can be interpreted as spirit communication always have a list of alternative explanations trailing behind them. It could be animals or*

*a person moving around outside, creaking floorboards,
static electricity, inadvertent knocks... The doubt is always
there for me.*

Yvette: *The tapping, banging and creaking were awesome.
At first the guys didn't believe me but I'm thrilled that
they heard the creaking too at the end. I'm very happy
with how this investigation went, but I'm also very happy
to be going home now. Initially when we first saw the
manor I was sad to see such a splendid place so run-
down, but I'm leaving with the feeling that this place
deserves that fate. Don't ask me to explain why I've
changed my mind, but I feel that some buildings are just
not meant to be cared for, because something so terrible
has happened in them that the memory of that event
can't be wiped away. They should just be left to fade away.
I believe the murder of that poor girl by the brothers all
those years ago may have created the sense of negativity
and evil aggression that I felt here. The more I think about
what happened all those years ago, the more a sinister
feeling comes over me. What is it that they say? Evil isn't
born, it is created. For me that sums up this place.*

A spooky postscript

Yvette: *Whenever I finish an investigation it's a great
relief to get home. It gives me a chance to reflect on
the night's events and try to relax. Sometimes it can
be difficult switching off, though, especially if the*

investigation was a particularly spooky one. On this particular night Ciarán and I had said our goodbyes and Karl and I went home. We were both exhausted when we eventually walked through our front door; we couldn't wait to get some sleep. It was only when we both climbed into bed that I heard tapping. I asked Karl if he could hear the thuds that seemed to be coming from under the floor. He looked at me as if I had completely lost my mind. I told him to listen carefully and sure enough, there it was again; this time we both heard three clear knocks. We couldn't believe it. Not in our house. Not now. We were both so tired. I decided that if I didn't respond to these noises Karl and I would be awake all night. I called out, 'Two knocks for yes, one for no. Who are you? Are you connected with this house?' We waited for a response but none came; there was just complete silence. 'Are you still here?' Karl asked. 'BANG' came the response. We continued to ask a variety of questions to ascertain who this spirit was but they clearly didn't want to tell us; all they would say, in yes-or-no knocks, was that they were there to protect us. Which is very nice, but I admit did make us feel a little uneasy, especially when we turned the lights out.

Ever since that night, if Karl and I call out questions, we often hear tapping in response. So maybe someone is watching over us; if so, we are incredibly lucky. When I told Ciarán of these strange events at home, his eyebrows darted towards heaven and he looked at me as if I were quite mad. Maybe I am . . .

3

The Liverpool Tunnels

Vaulted passageways cut out of solid rock: archways thrown up by craftsman's hands, beautiful in proportion, elegant in form, but supporting nothing. Tunnels formed here – deep pits there.

THE STREETS OF LIVERPOOL, J. STONEHOUSE

THE CASE OF THE LIVERPOOL TUNNELS

Under Liverpool's Edge Hill in north-west England is a mysterious underground labyrinth of winding tunnels and caverns. Over the years paranormal phenomena have been consistently reported here. Records show that the tunnels were built in the first few decades of the 1800s, and that the project was controlled by a somewhat eccentric retired tobacco merchant and philanthropist by the name of Joseph Williamson.

Williamson was born in 1769 and at a very young

age moved to Liverpool to lodge with his boss, Richard Tate, the wealthy director of a tobacco and snuff company. Joseph became rich through hard graft and working his way up through the company. He married the boss's daughter and later bought the Tate company from his brother-in-law. After making a great deal of money from selling the company, he built houses and dug out a network of tunnels and cellars beneath them all.

These houses, in the Kensington and Edge Hill districts of Liverpool, were oddly designed, with some featuring coal cellars on floors other than the usual basement or ground floor. Their location, however, in a part of Liverpool that was at the time highly desirable, meant that many rich people eagerly bought them up. Williamson died in the mid-1800s, leaving no children and, unfortunately, no clue as to his motivations for creating the tunnels. Following his death the tunnelling work ceased and most of the existing ones were filled with rubbish and left to decay.

There is a great deal of debate as to the purpose of the tunnels. A popular theory is that this is one of the earliest examples of a job scheme for the unemployed. Williamson was very conscious of his relatively poor background, and in the Liverpool of the 1800s witnessed a lot of extreme poverty; perhaps he felt the need to give something back. There are numerous other theories, each one, it has to be said, more outlandish than the last. They range from the tunnels being a manifestation of Williamson's extremely obsessive personality to his being a leader of a cult that believed in a coming Armageddon and building them as a subterranean hideaway for his followers.

Although some of the tunnels have caved in and become lost over the years, a lot of them do still exist today, underneath what is now a residential area, and in 2002 the Williamson Tunnels Heritage Centre reopened and renovated the tunnels as part of an ongoing exploration and redevelopment of Williamson's incredible legacy. Since then it is estimated that more than 50,000 people from all over the world have visited the tunnels and been amazed and fascinated by the scale and workmanship of Williamson's subterranean kingdom.

There's no doubt that the tunnels are fascinating from a historical, archaeological and sociological perspective, but the reason we decided to pay a visit in December 2006 was that over the years, and noticeably intensifying after the tunnels' 2002 reopening, there have been a number of alleged sightings of ghosts and unusual phenomena.

In addition to reports of people sensing various presences and hearing strange noises, visitors and workers in the tunnels have also reported ghostly sightings of the kind that respected local historian Tom Slemen describes below:

I went down the tunnels before they
were first officially opened, a long
time ago when I was a child, and had
heard of many alleged ghostly incidents
connected with these tunnels, including
an unseen 'ghost train' that was said
to run under Smithdown Lane, and a
ghostly procession of Irish navvies seen
walking down a tunnel of Crown Street
in the 1970s. The men were carrying
pick-axes and were walking in a line.

Since the tunnels reopened in 2002, staff say that a number of people visiting or working there have been startled by the apparition of a steam train and workers with pick-axes. A nine-year-old boy on a guided tour also recently reported seeing the figure of a man hanging by the neck at one of the tunnel entrances.

After reading the reports of hauntings in the tunnels, we couldn't wait to organise a visit. We spoke to representatives from the Heritage Centre and they kindly agreed to let us spend time alone in the tunnels without any staff members or other visitors present.

Our adventure begins

We arrive at the Williamson Tunnels' entrance and it is a bit anti-climactic at first because the tunnel entrance is totally characterless. It is hidden away in a residential area, near to Liverpool's Royal Hospital and Metropolitan Cathedral. There are rows of cars parked outside the houses, washing draped on lines between fences, litter on the pavements and toys strewn around small gardens. It all looks very ordinary; but as we've learned over the years, there really is no such thing when you're investigating the paranormal. Even the most mundane of settings can hold sinister secrets and uncover fascinating results.

As we walk towards the entrance we look over at some grassy wasteland, where a horse is grazing. For a moment we are transported back to the 1800s. We imagine horse-drawn carts delivering materials to the workers in the city's grime and dust. We see the workers' blackened, dirty faces as they leave the tunnels after a day's graft. This is our imagined impression of the dark, shadowy and claustrophobic work conditions of the nineteenth century, but we feel that the reality is waiting for us just beyond the tunnels' entrance.

We snap back to reality as we push open the swing doors and step inside. Staff waiting for us in the reception area greet us warmly and ask us if we are certain that we don't want anyone to accompany us into the tunnels, explaining that it can get very dark down there. We assure them that we are used to this kind of thing and that if we encounter anything we're not happy with we'll be sure to run back or yell for help!

In the reception area are displays of historical information about the tunnels and Joseph Williamson himself. While we kit up for the investigation, with equipment including torches, batteries, thermal imager and environment meters, we listen to one of the staff tell a fascinating story about Williamson's eccentricity – and what was perhaps his singular wisdom. The story goes that one evening he invited many of the local aristocracy and his influential friends to a meal in a cavernous room in the tunnel system. Once the guests were seated at the candlelit table, servants presented them with a meal of beans and meat of the sort regularly consumed by the tunnel workers. Most of the guests got up and walked out in disgust, complaining that they were of far too high standing in the community to eat such rubbish. The remaining guests were escorted into a different room, where Williamson sat waiting at a grand table on which an extravagant banquet was spread. He told them that they were the only dinner guests and true friends with whom he would willingly share this magnificent feast!

With respectful smiles for the man whose under-ground construction we are about to investigate, we open another set of swing doors and slowly make our way down into the darkness of the first underground chamber.

Our steps are tentative, partly out of sheer fear, partly for safety reasons. This first section of floor is a bit precarious and some loose gravel beneath our feet unnerves us slightly. We're in the first chamber now and it feels damp, and cold enough to see steam coming out of our mouths. We also note that there is virtually no air movement down here. Our eyes are taking a long time to adjust to the darkness so, because we can't really see where we are going, we walk very slowly and carefully. The light from our torches slowly reveals out of the blackness the beautifully crafted arched ceilings and, in stark contrast, scaffolding and dreary wooden flooring. Beyond us the tunnel opens up into an awe-inspiring and cavernous room. To the left, scaffolding supports a series of wooden steps and a gangway. About twenty feet down on the right is a dark, damp excavated section of tunnel, stretching away from us to the point where a towering brick wall blocks it. As we step on to the wooden gangway we can't help wondering if anything unusual will block our progress!

Ciarán: *At this point I'm feeling fine. I'm not frightened at all. Quite the opposite in fact; I feel very excited about just being in this location, and the possibility of seeing or experiencing something down here is a bonus. I feel very privileged that Yvette and I have been allowed down here unaccompanied. The blackness down here though is impenetrable. It is not like the countless renovated castles we've investigated at night, where there's always the option of pulling back curtains and letting moonlight flood in, or simply flicking a switch and 'let there be light'. When we switch off our torches in here, we are in total darkness. I really can't see a thing and Yvette is asking me to give her a stronger torch. I oblige but I also think it's necessary to put on my helmet with attached head-lamp. We need all the light we can get. I don't think I can remember ever being in such a dark place.*

Yvette: *I feel the same as Ciarán. I don't feel scared at all, just a little uncomfortable at the darkness but also excited. I also feel very fortunate to have the opportunity to explore without visitors, workers or tour guides present. Despite this it does feel a little surreal being here in this weird dark place. A second ago it was broad daylight and now there is nothing but total darkness. Darkness is actually an understatement, it is pitch-black. I need a stronger torch as I can't see where I am putting my feet. I can also hear dripping noises and they are a bit unsettling as the dripping isn't steady but irregular.*

We creep along the raised wooden gangway, grabbing the metal railing for security and peeking over the edge into the cavernous room below. As we edge our way along we are silent. Something about this impressive architecture seems to command an almost religious respect. The silence is suddenly broken by a loud crack. We stop dead, the torchlight no longer bobbing, our breathing momentarily frozen, then relax a little with a mutual nervous giggle and try to recreate the bang by retracing our steps. We try several times before discovering that our combined weight at a specific point on the gangway is what made the wooden plank emit the startlingly loud noise. Relieved, but also slightly disappointed, we stand still for a few minutes, soaking up the tunnel's atmosphere.

Yvette decides to call out. She recites an ancient incantation from Qabbala – that is, the esoteric theosophy of rabbinical origin based on Hewbrew scriptures from the seventh century, not the Kabbalah practised by certain celebrities of recent times. The incantation that Yvette uses is believed to energise and summon spirits, and after she finishes it she introduces herself and asks if there are any spirits or presences who wish to make themselves known to us. She also asks for a sign or a noise. We wait for a while, listening to the disconcerting and irregular dripping.

Yvette: *I've just called out, said an incantation and asked for a sign. I feel a little pessimistic as I feel we might need a medium down here to get anything. Or do we? Did you hear that Ciarán? I definitely heard something. It sounded like someone grunting. It isn't my imagination – I definitely heard it. I'm going to call out again. I can't believe this! I just felt two taps underneath my left foot. Ciarán tells me that he hasn't moved, so I wonder what that could be. This is very, very exciting for me as I really would like to get more phenomena like this without a medium guiding us.*

Ciarán: *Yvette is convinced we won't get much happening as we haven't got a medium present, but I remind her that the people who've reported phenomena here before are not mediums. Yvette is adamant that she heard a sound, but I haven't heard anything. She also tells me that she felt some tapping under her feet. I haven't moved so I know it's got nothing to do with me shifting my weight. Things are getting a bit interesting down here.*

Encouraged by the tapping, we decide to move further along the wooden platform. We're now at the end of the first chamber. Yvette continues to call out and Ciarán decides to have a go too. Yvette thinks she hears some quick, rapid footsteps, and asks Ciarán to run up and down the stairs to see if the sound is the same. It isn't. We continue to wait and watch in silence. At one point Ciarán is convinced that he sees something moving at the end of a small bridge, but after fiddling with his torch for a while he decides that it was a trick of the torchlight. Yvette looks down at her camera and is surprised that there is no dust on it, as there is a light covering of fine dust everywhere else. We continue to wait and watch. Neither of us is really sure what we are waiting for, but eventually our patience is rewarded when we both hear a low-pitched sound, something like a moan. Yvette asks Ciarán if he heard the noise and Ciarán replies that yes, he heard it and was waiting for her to mention it before he said anything. Both of us are sure that the other one did not make the noise, and our hearts start beating faster as we discuss the sound's characteristics and agree that it sounded very human – and very close.

Up until now we had been feeling fine, but in the last few minutes there has been a change of atmosphere and we're now both feeling uneasy. Given the choice of 'fight' or 'flight', right now we would definitely choose 'flight'!

The Fight-or-Flight Response

The human body reacts to danger on a very primitive level; the various physiological and psychological reactions, such as a speeded-up heart rate and that 'dry-mouth' feeling, that occur when we are scared or threatened have probably not changed in the whole long history of humankind. These physiological reactions are designed to prepare the body, to allow us to escape or defend ourselves against threats or predators. The fight-or-flight response is what makes us jump, scream, and want to run away in frightening situations. Psychologists who have studied fear, one of the most fundamental human emotions, have come up with an interesting theory as to why we scream when we are scared or startled. Firstly it is to scare the attacker, secondly it is a cry for help to anyone who may be nearby, and thirdly it functions as a warning to the rest of our social group. So, the next time you're in a haunted house and scream loudly because a cat leapt in front of you when you least expected it, don't feel silly. There's a perfectly logical reason for it and it is deeply human!

Our eyes are now to some extent accustomed to the dark, but we are still feeling apprehensive, thanks to the sensations in our bodies triggered by the fight-or-flight response. We reassure each other and take time to calm down a bit before moving on. The passage now winds its way up a few different levels via some more makeshift wooden steps. There are occasional holes in the wall that reveal small winding tunnels beyond, and dank obscured shafts that disappear into the dark. We come to a long tunnel with a left turn at the end, and what looks like temporary wooden walls and flooring. Although we're not actually scared – yet – the anticipation of what might be round the corner is starting to creep up on us. Towards the end of the tunnel, the temperature drops suddenly. Ciarán grins as he describes it as a 'classic cold spot'. Yvette walks through it and feels it for herself. The sensors are indicating the same thing.

Yvette: *For a second back there I was petrified. Hearing that moan reminded me of a similar awful experience at an investigation in the Golden Fleece pub in York. On that occasion I was the only one to hear the noise, a deep, spooky laugh, but here Ciarán heard the sound too. I'm sure it must have been someone, or something, trying to communicate. It really put me on edge when we started exploring further, and when Ciarán felt that cold spot I was jumpier than normal. It's fantastic, though, that we both experienced the cold spot, not just me.*

Ciarán: *That moan was fascinating. Sometimes I'd think that a sound like that could have been one of us clearing our throat or muttering in agreement, but neither of us had any recollection of doing anything like that, and the sound was rather different too. The possible problem is that as soon as we started talking about the sound we gave it a description – we both unintentionally encouraged each other to think of it as definitely being human in origin. It could have been one of us shifting our weight and causing the wooden flooring underneath to groan, but in ascribing 'humanness' to the sound, we were no longer able to keep any objectivity about it. The cold spot was also interesting as we both experienced it and it was confirmed by the monitoring equipment.*

As we step out from the tunnel into the second chamber, Ciarán points out that this is where the nine-year-old boy witnessed a graphic apparition of a hanging man. A sudden chill comes over Yvette as she realises the connection with the cold spot. On her instructions we stand still and Yvette calls out for the spirits to show themselves. We stand firm, ready to take pictures with our cameras, and with the digital video recorder on constant record. This is the moment in ghost-hunting that requires patience; if we had more time we would leave locked-off cameras here for at least a couple of hours. The tunnels here are open to the public though and so we have limited time to work. We complete the investigation by spending half an hour hoping to see a hanging apparition, then we leave one camera on a mini-tripod focused on the same spot and have one last walk around the entire tunnel system. None of the previously experienced phenomena happens again – with the exception of the cold spot. Ciarán takes some more readings around this area. We then start to make our way back to the entrance, and as we do Yvette is convinced she hears a slapping sound to her right. Her steps speed up. It's definitely time to go! For a brief moment of panic we both wonder which way is out . . .

Back Into the Light

Eventually we spot a shaft of light and follow it to the exit. As we walk down into this huge chamber we take a quick look at the display and the bits and pieces of crockery, some dating back to the 1800s, that were discovered when the tunnels were being renovated. It reminds us of the history of the place and how many people, some old and in poor health, would have lived, worked and died here in centuries past. We also notice the numerous oyster shells, cracked and stained by age, and Ciarán comments on how, centuries ago, oysters were not the expensive treat they are today; people would have been able to simply walk down to the banks of the River Mersey and harvest them out of the water.

We feel incredibly relieved to be out of the darkness and back in the comforting brightness of the reception area, although the intense feeling of being in the tunnels stays with us.

Leaving the door open so that light can shine through from the entrance, Ciarán returns to the first chamber to do some baseline readings. As expected, the humidity is between 65 and 70 per cent and the temperature of around 13.8°C is nothing unusual. The EMF readings are also normal. The only anomaly is the cold spot, although Ciarán thinks he may have a possible explanation for this. In fact, all the environmental measurements are normal, so we can't use them to explain any of the phenomena that have been reported here in the past, or the auditory phenomena that we feel we may have experienced ourselves.

Conclusion

Yvette: *This trip, like our trip to Allerton Tower, has really whetted my appetite for communicating with spirits without the use of a medium. Up until these two cases nothing really dramatic had happened to me without a medium or sensitive present to act as a focus. I used to wonder if it was Ciarán's scepticism and my lack of psychic or mediumship ability that blocked things, but after today I know this isn't true – we both heard something down there that is difficult to explain. It's also confirmed my belief that spirits don't discriminate between non-mediums or non-believers and those who do believe. I'm really excited! Delighted in fact, but as always I want us to be able to tell you that we have seen or heard more. I'm really looking forward to reviewing the tapes of our visit to the tunnels, in particular the moment when we both thought that each other had made a sound and it turned out we had both heard something. The taps under my feet were also memorable as I not only heard them but, more importantly, felt the vibration. All in all a really important investigation for me; it has strengthened my resolve to keep searching for the indisputable proof of life after death, with or without a medium present.*

Ciarán: *I'm excited about the investigation today as well. I definitely heard a strange sound and it is difficult after the fact to come up with a viable explanation. Even though I now describe it as a moan, it's hard to remember exactly what the sound was – it was kind of breathy, like someone clearing their throat or nasal passages – but was it human? I'm thinking through as many possible explanations as I can and the most probable is that when you're in a state of heightened awareness and concentrating on external noises, you are not fully conscious of noises you may make accidentally. Let's also remember that we may not always be aware that clearing our throats or breathing heavily would cause sufficient noise to be heard by someone else. It's frustrating as I have no definitive conclusion, yet, as to its origin. As for the cold spot, it could have been because the entrances and exits are not wind-proof and the spot is roughly halfway between the two. It's a long shot, but quick scans using the thermal imager do show a very slight air movement from both directions.*

Yvette is keen to initiate more communication like this without a medium present, but what exactly is a medium? It's interesting to note that the Fox sisters, who are credited with the creation of Spiritualism in the nineteenth century, never claimed to be mediums. Although there is debate about the sisters, doubt as to their credentials and whether or not they were frauds, the point I am making here is that Spiritualism didn't actually begin with mediums as we know them, but just with a group of people gathering together to witness strange phenomena. It was only later that mediums came on to the scene as the central character at many Spiritualist meetings. Also, for the two decades that I've spent immersed in psychical research, the majority of eyewitness accounts of hauntings have been sent to me by ordinary people who don't claim to be mediums or even 'sensitive' in any way. They are just people from all walks of life, like you and me, who believe they have witnessed something absolutely extraordinary.

Stanley Palace

4

Chester, an ancient city with roots reaching back to at least Roman times, has a reputation for being one of the most haunted cities in the UK, and we felt that *In Search of the Supernatural* wouldn't be complete without a visit to at least one of its allegedly haunted locations. We decided to visit Stanley Palace as it has been the subject of numerous paranormal investigations in the past, and many of these investigations had revealed interesting results. We hope ours will do the same!

THE CASE OF STANLEY PALACE

As you walk through the centre of picturesque Chester, you pass glorious Tudor architecture with steep roofs, large chimneys and the characteristic black-and-white half-timbering. This style of architecture is pretty familiar to us today, largely because it has been copied and revived over and over again; half-timbering was particularly popular in the nineteenth century, and styles copied from and inspired by Tudor buildings are also to be seen on many modern housing estates. Stanley Palace, however, is not modern; it's the real deal, a perfectly preserved Tudor mansion dating from 1591. The Stanley family, who came into possession of the house as a result of marriage, have their own exciting, florid, extraordinary history.

The house's and the family's story is especially fascinating around the time of the English Civil War, which ran from 1642 to 1651. James Stanley, the seventh Earl of Derby, did not keep his allegiance to the King quiet; even though it was dangerous to do so, he let it be known that he was a staunch Royalist. Towards the end of the Civil War one of his servants betrayed him to the Parliamentarians, otherwise known as the Roundheads. In 1651 he was arrested by the Roundheads and condemned to be executed. He spent his final traumatic and emotionally fraught days under house arrest at Stanley Palace.

Ironically, James Stanley's family had in the past stepped briefly into the ruling royal class, with his grandmother Lady Margaret Clifford being given honourable mention in Henry VIII's will. Indeed, the will stipulated that if she lived beyond 1603 she would be entitled to take the crown from Elizabeth I. Unfortunately she passed away in 1596.

The Stanley family tree reads like a 'Who's Who' of politicians and 'movers and shakers' down the centuries. Edward Smith Stanley, for example, held the post of Prime Minister of England three times in the second half of the 1800s. In 1892 another family member, Frederick Stanley, gave Canada a very special trophy – the Stanley Cup for ice hockey. Sound recordings also owe a debt of gratitude to Frederick Stanley. In 1888 his voice was heard on one of the first ever recordings of the human voice.

Over the years a number of ghostly presences have been witnessed in Stanley Palace. In addition, several amateur investigation groups have spent time accumulating evidence of ghostly phenomena, in the form of photos, recordings and witness statements.

There have been reports of one James Stanley roaming the hallway and rooms of the ground floor of what was once his mansion. The sound of children giggling and the apparition of a child have also been reported, as well as a gentleman dressed in some kind of uniform and a grey-haired lady playing the piano. Footsteps have also frequently been heard in the house's Long Gallery. In addition, a number of visitors, despite being alone in the building, have reported having a strong impression that there were other people in there with them. Of especial interest to us are the reports of chairs moving and vibrating as if of their own accord. On occasion these chairs have even been seen moving across the room. This is certainly something we will have to be extra-vigilant for as we carry out our investigation.

Home Alone: Our Investigation begins

It's December 2006, and we are standing inside Stanley Palace. It's the middle of the night, it's very dark, and only the two of us are here. The owners have given us the keys and permission to visit the house alone tonight. We know there is nobody in the house but us, and it's tremendously exciting as we wander around not knowing what to expect.

Yvette: *Ciarán knows a lot more about this house than me. I vaguely remember hearing something about vibrating chairs, but apart from that I am completely in the dark!*

Ciarán: *I'm going to call this our 'Scooby Doo' investigation! What I mean is that we have simply turned up here, in a place neither of us has visited before. Normally I like to check out a location beforehand in the daylight, mainly for safety reasons, but this time I decided to break that rule. I felt confident that it would be OK to do that as the house isn't that large and has been recently refurbished, so there won't be any dodgy floorboards to cave in under us.*

We walk through the entrance-hall area on the ground floor, and decide to begin the investigation by examining the house's upstairs rooms. Standing in front of the staircase though, as we're poised to head up to the first floor, we suddenly hear a loud crack. It stops us dead in our tracks and for a few seconds we are both silent. We had been quietly discussing how we felt about this place, but now we are rendered speechless. This was not one of those questionable little taps of the kind that we've encountered so many times before. This was a sudden, harsh noise right next to us. It sounded very much as if someone was coming down the stairs; it was so clear and so identifiable that we half-expect somebody to walk towards us.

We try to think of an explanation. Could it be the wind or a draft? This is an old house after all, so perhaps the floorboards are creaking? Feeling a little shaky, we decide to head upstairs to where the mysterious movement of chairs has been reported.

Yvette: *It's exciting having the place to ourselves. Although all the lights are off, I actually feel fine. At least, I did feel fine until I heard that loud crack. I'm used to waiting ages for something like that to happen and it just doesn't happen right away like that. The strange thing is that, although this house is old, it isn't a creaky place. It feels perfectly safe and the refurbishments are all finished. Also it feels 'settled'. By that I mean that Ciarán has told me that older buildings with wooden material like beams are not very likely to expand and contract and make noise, especially if they haven't changed over the centuries. They've had time to really 'settle'. I can't believe Ciarán's reaction – he normally remains very calm, but we were quietly talking and he just stopped with a surprised expression on his face. In fact, dare I say frightened?! It's great that the noise happened straight away, but I'm a little apprehensive now.*

Ciarán: *I feel like a kid in a candy store. As soon as we got permission to visit here I got very excited. I know that Chester has a reputation for ghosts and I know there have been lots of sightings here in Stanley Palace. There have also been some investigations by some practised amateur groups who have found interesting results. We are alone here, and we have the keys, so we know no one can get in or out. It's a calm night, so the bang can't have been caused by the wind. It could have been us walking on the floorboards but we've tried to replicate the sound and had no joy. I have no idea what caused it. I'm going to set up data loggers to read the temperature constantly whilst we're here. I'm also going to set up my EMF meter now to see if there are any unusual readings on the staircase, which is the focus of lots of reported activity. It is a wooden floor and perhaps static electricity has built up as a result of the heating and other electrical influences and appliances. If the static electricity suddenly discharged, it could create a loud banging noise and explain what we just heard. Great start though!*

Nervously, we both go upstairs and have a quick wander around. Although we have done countless investigations, seeing an unknown room in the dark, usually with tables and chairs and other everyday items scattered around, is always unnerving – that Mary Celeste feel, as if the place has been abruptly abandoned. Especially bearing in mind all those tales of chairs flying around! Noises from outside are much more noticeable up here than downstairs, and we can clearly hear the gentle hum of cars and conversation as people walk past. Although this is reportedly a very active part of the house in terms of unexplained goings-on, after a lengthy period of watching, waiting and calling out nothing has happened, so we decide to head back downstairs.

We check out a tiny cellar and storage room in the basement and also discover an exit door that leads to the main street. Everything seems very normal and quiet, and there are no reports of strange phenomena in these areas of the house, so we decide to have a wander around the whole building to properly famil- iarise ourselves with the layout of the place. This is rela- tively easy as Stanley Palace is smaller than we had expected. Feeling a little disappointed that we haven't experienced much after our successful, if scary, start with the bang, we go back upstairs to the first-floor living room.

We move two chairs and sit down in the middle of the room, facing the staircase. For quite a while we focus on some specific chairs – the ones that the owners have told us reportedly move of their own accord. We alternate our attention, focusing first on the chairs and then on the staircase, and set up a locked-off camera to film the whole staircase area, including the chairs. We are so focused, straining our eyes in the dark, that at times it looks to us as if a chair, or one of the other pieces of furniture, moves ever so slightly. Thankfully we will have the video footage to examine later in less tense circumstances. Then the silence is suddenly broken by a cracking sound. Ciarán is convinced that it came from upstairs but Yvette thought it came from downstairs or even from the stairs themselves; at first she thought Ciarán had clumsily bumped into a piece of furniture. We decide that as this is our first visit we need to spend more time getting to know the sounds of the house first to see if we can determine what is natural and what isn't.

We've now been sitting at the top of the stairs for about fifteen minutes in a total, tense silence, and have heard nothing. There are no repeats of the thuds or cracking noises that we heard earlier. We would like to be able to find out whether there's a rational explanation, for example that they were caused by the heating, but it's absolutely quiet. If it was the heating, surely you would expect the sounds to be regular and not random like that anyway?

Encouraged by the as yet unexplained cracking noise we heard earlier, Yvette decides to call out to see if any spirits want to make contact with us. She asks them to make a sound to let us know they are here. Ciarán also calls out that we mean no harm.

Yvette: *I'm feeling much colder here on the stairs but as Ciarán pointed out, this is probably to do with the fact that we are sitting still. I didn't feel this cold though when we were sitting on the chairs earlier, and we were sitting still then too. Ciarán has just told me that the stairs are a focus of alleged paranormal activity; so thanks for that! I was feeling jumpy before and now after those thudding sounds I feel really scared. I keep looking behind me at the chairs, thinking that they will move. There is the huge empty dark space of the living room, and the room beyond it, behind me. I know that open space is playing tricks on me. I'm going to put my camera down facing behind me in case anything happens. I don't have to look now behind me now, and I'm not sure I want to.*

Ciarán: *The loud cracks Yvette and I heard have mystified me as I have no idea what caused them. It can't be noise from outside as that sounds muffled and the noise we heard wasn't. It also wasn't the heating or the floorboards creaking or the sound of traffic outside, so what was it? Frequently sceptics, including myself, on hearing anomalous knocks and taps in an allegedly haunted location, point to the wooden structure of the building as a possible cause. Let me explain: the drop in temperature over the course of an evening could result in the wooden rafters contracting. This contraction, and its expansion again later when the temperature increases, could cause creaks and knocks and be misinterpreted as paranormal activity. That's the usual explanation I rattle off, anyway, but I've come to doubt it now after speaking to structural engineers and architects who have suggested that a building that has stood for hundreds of years could actually have adjusted to natural temperature fluctuations and be less likely to creak and knock than a more modern building. Yvette reminded me of this earlier on. I did notice, however, that there seems to be a faint source of heat – a heater switched off earlier in the day – behind a large wooden cabinet. The cooling influence may have caused a sound from the cabinet. Was the sound from upstairs or downstairs though?*

After spending close to an hour waiting and listening on the stairs, we decide to move on and investigate downstairs again. As we do we both agree that this investigation is an unusual one for us as we have no idea what to say or do next! It really is a waiting game for us both. There is nothing unusual to report on the ground floor so we cautiously head upstairs again, to the room where two blue wooden chairs have allegedly vibrated and even moved across the room. Once again we watch and wait but neither of the chairs moves. Disappointed, and conscious that time is running out, we decide to go downstairs for one last time to see if anyone or anything is lingering in this house.

We don't have to wait too long! No sooner have we entered the downstairs living room than we hear the same loud cracking sound that we heard earlier.

Yvette: *Wow! I feel really on edge now; those cracks are so spooky and so random. What is going on? We just need to sit down, be quiet and wait. It's a first for me and not at all easy, as I like to be up and doing something, keeping busy. This waiting game is the toughest part of ghost-hunting. If we brought our team here I'm convinced the place would come alive. What's that?! It sounded like a high-pitched whine and it was definitely coming from inside the building. My heart is in my mouth and I'm shaking.*

Ciarán: *It took a while but this is incredible. Yvette doesn't know this but there have been consistent reports here, over the years, of unusual visual and auditory phenomena. Both Yvette and myself have heard the cracks and now a whine and they were both loud and clear. It's great that I've heard everything too! Yvette is extremely perceptive when it comes to hearing unusual sounds in a location. Sometimes they may have a natural explanation, but there are other times when individuals can't hear them and yet on an audio recording they are there. I'm going to set a locked-off camera on the blue chairs to see if that picks up any movement while we're downstairs.*

Yvette calls out again, this time asking if the Earl of Derby is present and wishes to make contact. We hear what could be a dripping noise, but quickly realise that it is Ciarán's EMF meter making a sound as it resets itself every few minutes. Then we hear a huge bang from the stairwell and both of us turn towards it at the same time. We know from our earlier vigil on the stairs that it can't be the radiator pipes, the heating or noise from outside, so what on earth is it?

After a significant period of time we move upstairs to check on the locked-off camera. Even without checking the footage we know that the chairs haven't moved; we marked up their positions by placing little sticky labels by the legs, which show that they haven't budged an inch. There's one last thing that Yvette wants to try. She throws a coin to see if some sort of paranormal energy will roll it back towards her but, like the chairs, the coin stays very still although we sit and wait silently for half an hour. Everything seems to have gone very quiet, although from time to time as we wait in the darkness and silence we hear quiet, subdued noises coming from downstairs. If we didn't know better we would have sworn that someone was pottering around downstairs in their slippers.

Finally, Ciarán glances at his watch and announces that our time is up. It feels as if we've only been here a short while, but as things seemed to have settled down we reluctantly agree to call it a night!

Conclusion

Yvette: *Stanley Palace really was a waiting game. I'm glad we played it as we got some incredible thuds and loud cracks and even a high-pitched whine. I live in an old house and I've never heard cracks or thuds like that before. I'm always very aware of the knocks and taps that we get on investigations with a larger team but the sounds here were different. They were very loud and unexpected and almost sounded as though somebody wanted to get our attention. Bang! I'm here! It was annoying that we couldn't start communicating, getting regular bangs. Every investigation I do teaches me something and Stanley Palace is no exception. It's taught me that sometimes in an investigation the best approach is a laid back non-technical approach; you simply need to watch and wait and wait and wait.*

Ciarán: *There was no obvious natural explanation for the cracks and the thuds we heard (though I still suspect the heating upstairs and possible electrostatics downstairs), and like Yvette I was surprised that just the two of us working alone got such incredible results on our first visit. We did witness slight movement of chairs upstairs on our first vigil when we sat down and focused on them. Yvette and I discussed this as we packed up and walked back to the car, and I'm of the opinion that it was to do with our visual perception in low lighting. Without a point of reference and the slight light* reflection on the polished surface of one of the chairs, it could appear as though there was movement when in fact there was none at all. Yvette said to me that the best experience was the first loud crack, and I have to agree.

All in all it was very exciting indeed and, although I'm not one hundred per cent convinced yet, having spent some eerie hours there I'm not surprised that Stanley Palace has such a haunted reputation!

A Strange Postscript

Yvette and Ciarán have subsequently found out something compelling about James Stanley's grandson, who was also called James and who eventually became the tenth Earl of Derby. Yvette and Ciarán always say that their investigation into the Pendle Witches, a story that centres around Clitheroe in Lancashire, was their scariest ever. This later James Stanley, who was a politician, was elected to represent Clitheroe following the hanging of the Pendle Witches.

5

THE DEVIL'S ARSE

'Now to the *cave*, we come, wherein is found
A new strange thing, a *Village* under ground;
Houses, and *Barns* for men, and *Beasts behoof*
With distinct *Walls*, under one solid *Roof*.
Stacks both of *Hay* and *Turf*, which yields a scent,
can only from *Satan's* Fundament.'

FROM 'THE WONDERS OF THE PEAKE' BY CHARLES COTTON

Peak Cavern, or the Devil's Arse as it is otherwise known, is nestled in the Derbyshire Peak District, a part of the country that is renowned for its myths and supernatural legends. With so many eyewitness accounts and fantastical tales of spooky goings-on, it was only a matter of time before this location attracted our attention; so in November 2006 we decided to head up to the Derbyshire Peaks and pay a visit.

THE PARANORMAL IN PEAKLAND

Prior to our visit we did some research, and soon discovered that, in common with many places where alleged supernatural activity has occurred or is currently occurring, Peak Cavern, not to mention the Derbyshire Peaks surrounding it, has a long, fascinating and mysterious history.

We were originally attracted mainly to Peak Cavern itself, initially (we admit!) drawn in and amused by its nickname, but also very keen to find out the truth behind it and investigate the reports and rumours of ghostly experiences there. The sheer volume of supernatural stories we came across when researching the cavern and the surrounding area, however, made us think more about paranormal activity in the Peak District area in general, and about the links between local folklore and the many reported sightings of spectral beings. We came across more and more stories about unusual sightings, curious creatures and fantastical phenomena, as well as exciting legends deeply rooted in the fabric of local culture.

One story we kept hearing from locals was about a figure called Cock Lorrell (or sometimes Lorrel). We were intrigued and felt compelled to find out more about this character.

> *'Cocklorrel would needs have the Devil his guest,*
> *And bade him once into the Peak to dinner,*

Where never the fiend had such a Feast,
Provided him yet at the charge of a sinner.'
FROM *THE BALLAD OF COCK LORREL* BY BEN JONSON

Ben Jonson's ballad, written in 1621, is a satire on rogues and knaves from all levels of society. In it Cock Lorrell, also known as the Prince of Rogues, invites the Devil to Derbyshire for dinner. The dishes served up for the grand occasion are made from the bodies of people of various disreputable callings and hypo-critical habits.

'A rich, fat Usurer, stewed in marrow
With him a Lawyer's head and green sawce . . .
The sawce was made of yeoman's brains
That had been beaten out with his mace.
With a haydown, down . . . .'

Lorrell was allegedly the last king of the gypsies or beggars, and the 'most notorious knave that ever lived.' He is said to have presided over the large gathering of tinkers and beggars that was held annually in Peak Cavern in the late thirteenth century. Records show that the crown granted beggars the right to hold this feast in the cavern over a period of two weeks each year. By trade, Lorrel was a tinker, often carrying a pan and a hammer as a cover for his thieving. To this day, the word 'lorel' still means 'a sorry, worthless, fellow or good-for-nothing.' We were fascinated by this colourful character, and knew that this would be the first of many equally interesting stories that we would discover in the Peak District.

Storytelling

While researching folklore from Peak Cavern and the surrounding area, we realised that much of what we found out should be taken with a pinch of salt, as storytelling is always prone to the natural processes of exaggeration and deviation. It really struck a chord with us both, as we have learned over the years that accounts of ghost sightings must be regarded in a similar way. Although we're not saying that it's acceptable, or a good idea, to question the integrity of the witness or automatically assume that their account is pure fiction or highly exaggerated, it is very normal for someone recounting their experience of a paranormal phenomenon to highlight and exaggerate parts of their story, and generally to make the tale more colourful and compelling in an effort to convince the listener. Adding embellishments and excitement to a story is an intrinsically human trait. As well as the desire to make people believe us, other influences come into play, such as the teller's memories, as well as the influence of interruption, questioning or suggestion by listeners. All of these things may affect and distort the basic facts of the story, even if the teller is not consciously aware of them. Perhaps, then, many legends and myths started off as simple stories, which have become more and more elaborate after much re-telling over many years.

Derbyshire Ghosts

The Derbyshire Peak District is an area very rich in ghost stories. For a start there is a whole genre of tales of ghostly pedlars. A quiet lane near St Helen's Church in Darley Dale is sometimes referred to as Ghost Lane because of a pedlar whose ghost supposedly haunts it. Then there is the gruesome procession of twelve head-less phantoms that can supposedly be seen walking along Shady Lane near the village of Great Longstone. They carry a coffin and, so the legend goes, whichever unfortunate soul witnesses the procession may well be the occupant of the coffin next time round.

All sorts of spooky happenings have been reported in the area's caves and lead mines over the years. In the Goodluck Mine in the Via Gellia valley, a miner named Gamaliel Hall met his death hundreds of years ago. The initials G.H. can be seen to this day, carved into the rock; they are widely believed to be his, carved by his restless and probably resentful ghost.

The Peak District also has more than its fair share of haunted houses, pubs and castles. One of the most haunted buildings is allegedly Highlow Hall at Hather-sage, where apparitions of spirits have been reported for over six hundred years Precisely when the first ghosts date from is debatable, but there is an early tale of a female aristocrat who cursed her lover, one Nicholas Eyre, for cheating on her, and then commit-ted suicide. Another wandering spirit at Highlow Hall is said to be that of a stonemason, caught idling by the same Nicholas Eyre and punished for it by death. In another murder case from history, two drunken men had a fight and one of them pulled a sword, killing the other. The dead man's ghost is said to wander the Hall's grounds, perhaps still seeking revenge. Staff have also reported seeing a pale lady enter the front door of the hall.

Winster Hall, in the village of the same name, is said to be haunted by two lovers who, rather than be separated, made a suicide pact and leapt off the roof. Taddington Hall in Taddington village is also reportedly home to the ghosts of two former, though rather less tragically romantic, residents. One is a drunken farmer who fell from his horse on his way home from market in Bakewell. His wife reported at the time what is called a 'crisis apparition'; in other words, his ghost appeared to her either at the exact time his death or very shortly before it happened. The other ghost at Taddington is of a rather mysterious figure known only as Isaac, who is said to have been murdered by his brother in the Hall's cellar.

Too Much to Drink?

The Derbyshire Peak District seems to be especially rich in ghosts who haunt one particular type of building – pubs! We decided to visit some – in the name of doing our research, of course!

The Travellers Rest pub at Brough is supposedly visited by the ghost of a farm girl who died after falling headlong down the stairs while fleeing a drunken admirer. Supernatural happenings at the Red Lion, Wirksworth involve a coachman who literally lost his head as his horses, out of control, galloped under a low archway.

The ghosts of children are said to haunt the Miners' Arms pub at Eyam. Reportedly, some long-ago local children accidentally started a fire in the wooden shack that then stood on the spot. The shack also covered up an old and, until then, forgotten mine shaft. In the ensuing panic of the blaze, one child died in the fire and a little girl fell down the mine shaft. Regulars in the pub have reported hearing mysterious noises and also poltergeist-like phenomena involving objects moving of their own accord, or under the control of a mischievous or disruptive spirit.

We wanted to spend a bit of time soaking up the atmosphere of a haunted pub, so late one afternoon we headed to the Castle in Castleton, a pub that we chose because of its association with a tragic local love story.

Ciarán: *Yvette and I have sat down in a corner of the pub and ordered a drink and a bite to eat. It was here that a group of unscrupulous men made the plans that eventually led to the murder of a young couple over money. I'm not sensitive, in the spiritual sense, in any way and yet, sitting here, aware of what happened, I'm gripped with both anger and sadness. Yvette has just gone quiet and, for a moment, the lively murmur of the pub's customers suddenly just died away too.*

Yvette: *This is a very unusual setting for me for so many reasons. My family and I occasionally treat ourselves to weekend lunch in a pub, so aside from the fact I'm sitting here on a weekday without my family here, there are other, more supernatural reasons as to why this is unusual. I've done so much hunting of ghosts that following on the trail of other supernatural phenomena, be it mystical creatures, gypsy kings or any other legend, is a new experience for me. I'm so used to sitting in a darkened castle and calling out for spirits that this style of investigation is quite refreshing. Ciarán says I have to get my research hat on and become a bit bookish! One thing's for sure though, sitting here and letting your imagination run wild, trying to picture the scene all those centuries ago, is something I can do. Even though it is 2006 and the conversations in other parts of the pub are about modern-day things like television and music, I can easily imagine the place being pretty much the same back in the 1700s. People would have been drinking, laughing, gossiping then too. But I'm now starting to think about the tragic young couple who have popped in for a drink, unaware of what will happen to them, unaware of the men sitting talking about them. I don't feel like talking right now. Also,*

Ciarán has just told me about what's supposedly buried under the front door, believed by pagans in times past to be a good-luck charm – the body of a young woman. Okay, now I'm spooked, let's talk about something else, or get out of here!

Our conversation turns to rather lighter topics as we consider the Peaks and the huge variety of fascinating and mysterious things that they no doubt hold in store for us. We get onto the topic of Unidentified Flying Objects or UFOs. As if the ghost stories and the rich and strange tales from folklore and local legend weren't enough, the Peak District has quite a history of these bizarre sightings too.

Lights Over the Moors

Out on the moors and fells that the pubs provide shelter from, supernatural and unexplained activity is apparently rife. There are numerous accounts from walkers and climbers in the Peak District of encounters with inexplicable lights.

Typically this phenomenon is described as the sighting of a glowing ball, or balls, of light whose movements are often described as defying natural explanation. They may stop suddenly in their tracks, move at a snail's pace, or accelerate to speeds that appear to be beyond the capabilities of anything manmade. These lights are sometimes referred to as ghost lights, and are often said to be due to a tragedy that took place at the location they are seen in.

A number of more rational explanations for the lights have also been put forward, ranging from car headlights and naturally occurring phosphorescence to shifting geological plates and natural radioactivity from the earth. Some sightings of lights, such as the famous Marfa Lights in Texas, the Brown Mountain lights in North Carolina, the Hornet Spook light in Missouri, and some sightings here in the Peak District, remain unidentified, true mysteries still.

After our conversation, intrigued by the possibility of encountering some mysterious lights, we take a leisurely drive away from the safety of the towns and villages and head out beyond Castleton into the higher peaks. Out here you feel truly alone and it's easy to imagine getting lost and encountering something supernatural. Stopping the car briefly to get our bearings, and looking across at the farmland stretching before us, we see sheep grazing. The light is now fading and shadows start to creep across the fields. Then all thoughts of spotting strange lights in the sky leave our heads as suddenly, out of the corner of our eyes, we both glimpse movement beside a stone wall; a small dark shadow that looks like an animal runs past.

Yvette: *I feel like I'm on the set of* An American Werewolf in London. *I'm thinking about the opening scenes when the two Americans are warned, 'Stick to the path lads, stick to the path'. They then accidentally wander off on to the moors, only to face a fearsome creature. The countryside here is absolutely stunning, but at the same time there is a slight undeniable creepiness about it. We both saw a shadow, first crouching down and then suddenly running out of view. It could easily have been a small furtive animal, a fox maybe or a cat, or even a dog, but it was unnerving. No doubt we'll have forgotten about it by tomorrow but it has made us both think about the many reported sightings of larger, more bizarre animals in the area.*

Boggarts and Black Dogs

One of the most unusual legends associated with the Derbyshire Peak District is that of a giant black dog known as the boggart. Eyewitness accounts have described this creature as being the size of a calf, with a shaggy black coat and glowing eyes as big as saucers. It never makes a sound and always vanishes as quickly as it appeared, as if into thin air. A little bit of research threw up many and varied descriptions of these boggarts. We read accounts of spirits that act as warnings and goblins that prey on farmland. We were fascinated by the notion of the boggart and wanted to find out if we were dealing with a variation on the 'Black Dog' sightings that are reported as occurring all over the UK. Ciarán tracked down Dr Simon Sherwood, a parapsychologist based in Northampton who is also one of the UK's leading experts on the Black Dog phenomenon.

Q(Ciarán): *First of all can I ask, what are Black Dogs?*

A(Simon S): They are dog-like apparitions but they differ from normal dogs in the sense that they are usually bigger, their eyes are bigger than normal dogs' and they behave differently to normal dogs. For example they might seem to disappear or fade from sight. To some folklorists, so-called Black Dogs can also be other colours.

Q: You do actually use the word 'apparition', so we're not talking about just big, black dogs, is that right?

A: No, we're talking about dogs with different character-istics. People may think they are seeing a normal dog when they first encounter it, but usually the creature fades away from sight, or vanishes, or goes through a brick wall for example. It does the kind of things a normal dog can't do, but an apparition can.

Q: Aside from the size and eyes do Black Dogs have any other identifying characteristics?

A: Often people describe the eyes as red or yellow, and frequently they say that they are glowing or fiery. Sometimes the eyes can be as big as saucers. In some reports the dog can change shape. In one account, for example, it was reported to change shape into a donkey! Or, in another case, it changed into human form. There are also cases where the dog can shrink in size, or gradually get bigger and bigger. There are a few cases also where the dog supposedly grinned at the person.

Q: Can these sightings happen to anybody?

A: Yes, definitely. The earliest case I'm aware of was twelfth century. Later there was the famous case of the Black Dog of Bungay in 1577, and of course people are still reporting them today. The latest account I have is probably from about two years ago. So it can happen to all kinds of people in all kinds of locations.

Q: That was my next question – do you hear of cases all over the world or is this just an English phenomenon?

A: In terms of folklore it's understood to be a distinctly English, or British, phenomenon. But I've got cases from elsewhere in Europe, Australia, North America. There's a book that's recently come out, giving accounts of Black Dog sightings in Latin America. So, from my perspective, it's certainly more than a British phenomenon. Another notable thing is that cases are often associated with a particular location, for example a bridge, monument or certain road. These are more the 'haunting' type cases as opposed to the one-off eyewitness reports.

Q: What is your take on the Black Dog phenomenon? Do you have any explanations or do you prefer to keep an open mind?

A: The thing that intrigues me about Black Dogs is that they are so different to other hauntings. Seeing an apparition of someone you know is perhaps 'normal' for want of a better word, whereas Black Dog apparitions are more of a challenge to the theories of hauntings and ghosts generally. I don't think we're in a position yet where we have one explanation for apparitions anyway. There are so many different types and Black Dogs are one such type. There could be one explanation for some sightings of Black Dogs but not for others and the same explanation may not apply to humans.

Q: Is it true that you had an experience that started all of this research?

A: Yes, I saw a Black Dog in my bedroom when I was about ten years old. It was a massive black creature and was galloping towards me. Its eyes were bright yellow and as big as saucers. It disappeared the second it got to my bedroom door. It was terrifying and at the time I couldn't scream or shout. It was that and reading about a similar case in the local paper that got me interested in the topic.

Q: Looking back on that experience can you explain it?

A: I have done research on hypnagogic and hypnopompic imagery, the states between waking and sleeping, as well as sleep paralysis. I think this is one alternative explanation for my experience especially considering I was in bed at the time, but it doesn't convince me completely that there is a psychological explanation for them. You do find people reporting experiences when they're very unlikely to be asleep. The fact that the majority of sightings occur outdoors supports this. As with apparitions generally, we need to know a lot more about the characteristics of Black Dogs and the circumstances under which they're seen before we can fully draw conclusions. I don't think we have an explanation for them yet.

Q: We've been doing some research around the Derbyshire Peaks looking at all manner of things supernatural and one of the things associated with the area is something called a 'boggart'. There are a variety of descriptions of boggarts, everything from a domestic spirit to agricultural goblins! But we have come across some tales of boggarts described as black dog-like creatures. We've seen them described as large dogs bigger than a calf with characteristics such as a shaggy coat, glowing eyes, and having the ability to disappear quickly. What do you make of that?

A: It's interesting, though I'd last heard the name 'boggart' in Harry Potter. I think it was described as a shape-shifter. The first descriptions of boggarts, the spirit and goblins, don't match the typical Black Dog, but the other descriptions do have the same characteristics. In fact, in Yorkshire, the Black Dog is known as a barghest, which isn't a million miles removed, linguistically, from boggart, so I wouldn't be surprised if you've found yourself another case of the Black Dog phenomenon.

A related cryptozoological phenomenon (cryptozoological is the technical name given to research into creatures from legend and myth) is the werewolf. This is a creature that has long been associated with the Derbyshire Peaks. There are numerous accounts, going back hundreds of years, of eyewitnesses reporting sightings of animals resembling a wolf or large dog. Perhaps some of these 'werewolf' sightings are actually Black Dogs? We have also learned that boggarts are sometimes believed to act as messengers of impending danger. For example, there are historical accounts of miners seeing Black Dogs and, believing them to herald a disaster or accident, refusing to go down into the mines. Other miners who ignored or were cynical about a Black Dog and went down to work in the mines as normal would sometimes suffer an accident, often a fatal one, down there.

The Case of the Devil's Arse

Finding out about the amazing legends, history, folklore and alleged paranormal activity reported at or near Peak Cavern (to give it its official name) made us very eager to explore, interview and investigate for ourselves. Unfortunately, due to safety hazards and concerns we were only permitted to enter the cavern as part of a guided tour, so this investigation was more limited than others, but as you will see it still yielded some fascinating and thought-provoking results.

On New Year's Day 1999, previous records tumbled when cavers broke through into the bottom of a chamber and scaled it to a height of 500 feet, thus discovering the tallest known chamber in Britain and impressively eclipsing the 330 feet of the previous record-holder, Gaping Gill in North Yorkshire. As well as its incredible, record-breaking physical size, Peak Cavern is also historically and culturally one of the most important cave systems in the UK. It is right underneath the ruins of a Norman castle that was built in 1086 by one William Peveril, a favourite knight of William the Conqueror. In fact, Peak Cavern is mentioned in the Domesday Book, and Peveril Castle, which sat on top of it, is described as 'Castellum in peches ers', meaning 'The castle on Peak's rump'. The area as it was in those days was described as 'The Royal Forest of the Peak, where nobles hunted bears, wolves, deer and wild boar.' This got our minds racing. Would we find some wild animals on our visit? Or perhaps something more sinister?

Some of the history of the Devil's Arse is, unsurprisingly, mingled in with that of Peveril Castle, which changed hands many times down the centuries until, in 1932, it was acquired by the then Duke of Devonshire. Records show that from the seventeenth century until the 1970s, Peak Cavern was, incredibly, home to successive generations of rope-making families, who built their machinery and their dwelling places inside and lived, worked and died there. Bert Marrison, the last Peak Cavern ropemaker, who retired from the work in 1974, is recorded as saying that the Duke of Devonshire let the ropemakers use the cavern rent-free 'whilst ever there was a master or his apprentice working there.' Mr Marrison remembered, in his youth, thirty people working in the entrance in their family businesses. Although all this is gone now, modern-day visitors to the cavern can still watch a demonstration of rope-manufacturing techniques.

In the seventeenth century, well-to-do travellers were encouraged to visit the cavern and its cave-dwelling community; it became well known as a 'must-see' on any Grand Tour of Derbyshire. It seems that the resident ropemakers always welcomed the opportunity to leave their work for a while and act as guides to these curious tourists, but the visitors often needed 'emboldening' to visit this twilight world inhabited by what writers of the time have described variously as 'human moles', 'troglodytes' and 'beggars' who lived in 'little styes'. Because of the cavern's low ceiling, once they were in visitors would have to be ferried across the water lying down, making the experience even more atmospheric, memorable, and no doubt eerie.

The following suggests that by the closing decades of the 1700s, organisers of the trip into the Devil's Arse had decided that it should be a somewhat less Gothic experience, and put the emphasis on rather lighter entertainment:

. . . at this place you are entertained by a company of singers who have taken another path and ascended to a place called the Chancel, considerably higher than the party you stand on, where with lights in their hands they sing various songs. The effect is very striking.

WILLIAM BRAY, 1778

Despite the efforts of the singers and their lights, though, the Devil's Arse seems to have retained down the centuries a reputation for and atmosphere of threat, or at least of a certain uncanniness.

It has certainly long been thought of as a doorway to somewhere strange, if not decidedly otherworldly; perhaps one of the most romantic stories of all those associated with the cavern was written down around the year 1211 by a writer and statesman by the name of Gervase of Tilbury to amuse his patron, the Emperor Otto IV. He describes the notorious peak's hole and claims that stormy winds sometimes blow from the cavern. He tells of a pig farmer who believed he had lost one of his sows to the otherworld beyond the cavern. The farmer was afraid of the cavern but also feared the consequences from the Lord of Peveril Castle should he not find the animal. He entered the cavern in a desperate bid to find the sow, scared out of his wits and wondering if he would ever return. Surprised to see a source of bright sunlight deep in the cavern, he continued on and came across the incredible sight of bountiful summer fields ready to be harvested. The farmer was greeted by the ruler of this strange summer land under the earth and, after finding his sow, had to ask for permission to return to his world. Having been granted permission by the otherworldly ruler, the farmer navigated his way through the cavern back to the wet miserable weather of an earthly British winter.

We thought this sounded like an incredible, fantastical story. But who knows! Would we find ourselves in another world too when we investigated the cavern?

Another connection between dark evil forces and Peak Cavern (which at one time was also called 'Auld Horney', which is a nickname for the Devil) can be found two miles away. On a hillside, above forest, is an open pot-hole some 180 feet deep, called Eldon Hole. According to local legend an old woman's goose fell down Eldon Hole. It emerged from Peak Cavern three days later, its tail singed but otherwise unharmed.

And finally, folklore and legend aside, there's

another explanation as to how Peak Cavern earned its saucy nickname and its dark association with the Devil; the strange noises and cracks that can be heard from within. After heavy rainfall, parts of the cavern fill up with water. When the water subsides it gets sucked up, along with air, into various crevasses within the cave system. It is a similar principle to sucking on a straw as you get towards the end of your drink. The process results in loud noises that often sound like tremendous farts – hence the name the Devil's Arse.

Into the Devil's Arse

It's a cold November morning in 2006 and we are travelling by car to Peak Cavern. We purposely take the route through Winnats Pass because we've been told by locals that the name Winnats means 'wind gates', and that all sorts of meanings and interpretations are ascribed to the sound of the wind that blows through this lonely pass. According to local lore, some are the ghostly screams of the two runaway lovers from the 1700s who were robbed and murdered here, schemed against by the unscrupulous group of men in the Castle pub. We found an account of what happened to the doomed couple – and what later happened to their attackers – on the website of Peakland Heritage.

The runaway lovers died together in the Winnats Pass but divine justice lent a hand in punishing their five murderers. The young couple, remembered only as Allan and Clara, were riding to Peak Forest to be married at the famous 'runaway church'. The lovers had travelled a long way, arriving at Castleton in the dark. They stopped briefly at a local inn, where a group of lead miners noticed that they were carrying a bag of money. Allan and Clara resumed their journey but as they rode through the Winnats Pass were robbed and murdered by the five men. Their bodies were hidden and not discovered for many years. The murderers however met with divine justice. One broke his neck in the Winnats; a second was crushed by a fall of stone; a third committed suicide; a fourth died mad and the fifth made a death-bed confession. You can still see Clara's red leather saddle in the shop of Speedwell Cavern, at the entrance to the pass.

Our hearts skip a beat as we navigate round the steep curves. Winnats Pass is a busy and a modern place, cars speeding past in both directions, and we don't see Allan or Clara or hear their ghostly screams, but we do decide to stop at Speedwell Cavern, at the base of Winnats and just up the road from Peak Cavern. It is here that we see Clara's red saddle on display, a bittersweet and melancholic sight.

Yvette: *We've just seen Clara's saddle and it's put me in the right mood to follow on their trail. I suggested to Ciarán that we climb up Winnats Pass a bit. Driving down it was a bit scary for our first time and I didn't really have a chance to take in everything around me.*

Phew, this is quite a climb, I daren't look down yet, at least not until my feet are firmly planted. We're at a high point now and from here the view is stunning. I can see the car parked below us at Speedwell and the village of Castleton beyond. It was about here that the men who killed Allan and Clara would have hid, watching the couple as they rode up Winnats Pass. I can sense their cruel steely eyes and dark, immoral presence. There's a real sense of anticipation here. It feels as though Ciarán and I are just about to leap out from behind the little brow where we're hiding now and run down the hill. There are a couple of tourists around here and they must be looking up at us wondering what on earth we're doing crouching down behind the hilltop.

Ciarán: *Standing at this point on Winnats Pass it's easy to see how the murder may have played out. Allan and Clara were ignorant of the pack of men following them; the men were probably miners and farmers who knew the lie of the land, so were able to approach stealthily. The murderers would undoubtedly have discussed Winnats Pass in their plan of attack, knowing that the high ground would give them the advantage. From up here you can see the approach from every compass point, and make sure that nobody is around before making the run down the slope to where the innocent couple would have been accosted. Yvette is starting to feel a bit uneasy now and also getting a bit angry at what transpired here. I'm going to let her soak in the atmosphere for a bit before suggesting we go. From my perspective I think her soaking up the atmosphere is the explanation for Yvette's feelings. She has a vivid imagination and is really placing herself in that scenario and it's unnerving her. Time to leave.*

We drive down to Peak Cavern and find a place to park. A short riverside walk takes us past centuries-old miners' cottages before leading us out into a spectacular limestone gorge. Ahead of us we glimpse for the first time the 280-foot-high vertical cliffs, with the ruins of Peveril Castle towering above. It's yet another one of those 'wow' moments for both of us!

Gary, our friendly and extremely well-informed tour guide, meets us at the entrance. He takes us slowly and carefully into the entrance chamber, and as we enter we take a good long look at the remains of the village where that community of ropemakers lived and worked for more than 400 years. The mechanisms have been restored, and we pause for a while as Gary gives us a brief rope-making demonstration and then talks about the awesome stalactites hanging down in menacing shapes from a cleft in the roof. We ask about the shapes and Gary explains that stalactites are formed by slightly acidic water dissolving small amounts of limestone as it filters down through tiny fissures in the rock. When this water reaches the roof of the cave, the water drops away and the dissolved limestone is left behind. Over many thousands of years this deposit accumulates into a stalactite and some of these formations take on a recognisable shape. One characterful stalactite, for example, is the 'Flitch of Bacon' – it resembles half a pig hanging up – and another looks very like an old man.

Walking down to the end of the vestibule where the path dips down to a little chamber called the Bell House, we meet the cave air for the first time. We notice that it feels quite warm and Gary tells us that the temperature here remains constant all year round at 9°C, so that it feels cool in summer and quite warm in winter. He also tells us that it is here that storm water rises to the roof and flows round the back of the ropewalks and out of the main entrance. It is when these storm waters recede that water and air are sucked forcefully down a tight siphon, resulting in the loud farting sound mentioned earlier that earned the cavern its nickname. Gary asks us to bend down very low to make our way down a short walk – appropriately named Lumbago Walk – to reach a little pond called the Inner Styx. Years ago, he explains, the only progress from this point was to lie flat in the straw-covered floor of a boat as a guide pushed you under the low arch into the Great Cave. Many eminent visitors were once brought into the cavern in this manner – Queen Victoria is said to have visited the cave in 1842 and, if so, would have to have been shoved through the arch in this way.

After emerging from the tunnel we enter the Great Cave and are told that it is 150 feet wide, 90 feet long and 60 feet high, a quite remarkable size. We trace with our fingertips the centuries-old lines and holes on the limestone, marks from the water that have hollowed out the cave over the millennia.

It's time to move on again, and we walk up a high pass to a rock formation named Roger Rain's House, where there is a perpetual cascade of water. A balcony high on the rock wall is lit up and Gary explains that this is the Orchestra Chamber. In times past, wealthy travellers were entertained from that balcony by the village choir. The final chamber we enter is called Pluto's Dining Room; from there a wide flight of stairs called the Devil's Staircase lead visitors back to daylight. On the rock wall of the staircase can be seen the names of artists, poets and writers, Lord Byron among them.

Gary tells us that we really have only scratched the surface of the caves, but that the far depths are only suitable for exploration by experienced cavers with the right equipment. We ask if before we leave we can at least experience total darkness in the cave, and he obliges by turning the lights off.

Ciarán: *There is no source of light anywhere here. It is not even the case that some light in another part of the cavern system could leak through. We are so far into the cavern that no light is seeping through at all. I'm suddenly reminded of a scene in the film* Pitch Black, *a piece of science-fiction that features a group of people* stuck on a planet where carnivorous flying creatures allergic to light hunt their prey in darkness. There's a scene where the group, fleeing the monstrous creatures in the dark, manage to keep them at bay and survive by surrounding themselves with lights. One of the lead characters gets separated from the group and loses his torches. He is in total darkness until he pulls out a lighter and flicks it on, only to be confronted by a circle of the hungry razor-teethed beasts. As the lighter is slowly extinguished, the viewer can't see anything. We just hear the screams . . . I look into the darkness and shiver as a chill runs down my spine. I switch my torch on momentarily just to calm myself down. Yvette tells me off. It's amazing how darkness can start to play tricks with your imagination.

Yvette: *This is really scary. I know the size of the place and yet with the lights off I really can't picture it. I can't see my hands or Ciarán standing next to me. Is he standing next to me? I can hear a slight shuffle. I hope it is him! There's definitely a sense of presence here. I don't know if it's because of the stories we've heard of children centuries ago running up into the rocks and either guiding paying tourists or playing games in there, but I'm feeling like we're being watched. Little beady eyes seem to be darting behind rocks above us. I keep expecting a stone to come flying past. What was that? Oh, Ciarán turn your torch off. That was enough to give me a heart attack! Don't do that again. I'm going to call out briefly. Our guide probably thinks I'm crazy but, hey, this is what I do! There's no response but I still feel like we're being watched. Either the spirits are stalking us or the cave is, keeping a careful eye on our progress. This anticipation is killing me now. The eyes are now burning into my back and I'm ready to leave.*

Yvette is keen to leave but Gary tells us that some of the cavers and divers who work in the caves are ready to talk to us about their experiences down here, so we make our way to the cave entrance to meet them.

While we wait for the cavers Yvette tells us that she sensed something unpleasant down in the cave when the lights were off. Gary tells her that her experience is not unusual; many visitors have told him they have felt the same thing, and there have been instances when he has felt freaked out too. We haven't got time to talk any more, because the cavers and divers have arrived and we're keen to hear about their experiences.

We greet the group and Yvette starts to grill them for information. Perhaps surprisingly for such scientifically minded people, all of them are very open-minded about the possibility of paranormal activity in the caves and almost all say that they have heard or sensed things over the years that they can't explain.

One caver tells us that he has often heard the sound of children crying, when he knows that he is well out of earshot of the cave entrance with its crowds of visitors. We ask if he believes in ghosts and he tells us that he doesn't think so, because for him 'seeing is believing' and he has never seen one. But he goes on to say that he would be a 'liar' if he didn't admit to feeling spooked from time to time when he is working alone in the caves.

Another caver steps forward. He tells us that sometimes for no reason at all the 'hairs on the back of his head' will stand on end and he feels as if someone is with him. He says he stops working if that happens, and waits for the feeling to ease off. He is sure it isn't psychological, as the next day he is always fine. It is then that he tells a tale of disaster forewarning, a type of tale we learned of earlier in our visit to the Peak District, and one that we had assumed was simply a story that used to be told by miners centuries ago.

```
On one occasion I believe a strange
feeling of being watched saved my life.
A few years back I was in a cave
system not far from here. I felt a
little apprehensive, like I was being
watched, and I kept on hearing a
strange banging noise. My pack also
kept getting stuck on a ledge and I
couldn't understand why so I decided to
leave. Later I found out that if I
hadn't decided to leave at that moment
I would have been buried a few hours
later under a rock fall.
```

The caver also says that most of his fellow cavers report feeling uncomfortable when they work on their own in a chamber. We ask if he is ever afraid and he tells us he isn't, because his peers here often talk about feeling that there's someone 'looking out for them'.

Sadly, we have run out of time and have to prepare to leave, but we aren't going away from here empty-handed; we've got an awful lot of rich and fascinating material to work with.

Conclusion

Ciarán: *It was fascinating for me to visit Peak Cavern. It is a truly unique natural phenomenon, rich in history and legend, but do I believe it is haunted? Although I can appreciate why the Devil's Arse has a mysterious reputation and, as always, I'm keeping an open mind, I'm not entirely convinced that it is. I'll explain my reasons.*

Centuries ago, when people's understanding of the world was based on their religious beliefs rather than scientific knowledge as we know it today, any natural phenomenon that people couldn't understand or explain tended to be attributed to the Devil. For example, even the seemingly innocuous fossilised remains of a common oyster-like creature called Gryphaea arcuata, *because of its resemblance to a gnarly curled nail, was given the name the Devil's Toenail. It is hardly surprising in such a culture that a huge, mysterious and awe-inspiring* cavern, surrounded by impressive but forbidding cliffs, should attract fascination, fear and superstition – and the nickname the Devil's Arse.

That name is an important ingredient too. It played on my imagination before I visited it, so I can totally appreciate how it must have built anticipation in the minds of other visitors, both past and present, perhaps creating something of a feeling of fear and dread even before they arrived. Of course the cave has always had an association, not just with the Devil but also with the outlandish figures of beggars and thieves, personified by that delightfully romantic and deviant character Cock Lorrell. The belief that it was a place of social transgression and scandal must have added another frisson in the minds of its visitors.

Those long-ago tourists would have travelled, sometimes a long way, over Derbyshire's wild and desolate moors to get to the cavern, passing under the fearsome vertical cliffs on their way to the enormous gloomy cave itself. Here they would have met the poor and ragged ropemakers who worked in 'God's factory'. In those days many people rarely left their own town or local area, and so they wouldn't have been familiar with the workers' dialects and mannerisms and would probably have considered them very strange and eccentric. Consider also that the people who lived in the caves would probably have been surrounded by, to the eyes of the wealthy visitors, considerable squalor – sooty fires, discarded food waste and bodily waste from both *themselves and their animals. It's not really surprising then that accounts from those days describe the people they saw as 'human moles' and 'troglodytes'. In the cavern itself, people would have been overawed by the size and gloom inside the chambers and the oddly shaped stalactites. Without the understanding we have now of how these natural phenomena are formed, their imaginations must have run wild and ascribed all kinds of supernatural explanations to the existence of this place.*

Given all this I can fully appreciate why people in times past feared the caves, but what about modern-day visitors and cavers? Why do some continue to report feeling spooked? Having visited the place myself I can again see why. Ancient castle, legends, werewolves and folklore aside, nature has created an awesome and eerie spectacle at the Devil's Arse that can't fail to inspire both wonder and fear. As you wander through the caves in semi-darkness, with the gentle sound of water trickling in the background – and, if you're lucky, the cavern's famous noises – it's very easy for the imagination of even the most sceptical paranormal investigator to start to run wild.

As for the cavers, their experiences could be explained away by the long hours they spend working alone in the darkness, and their minds playing tricks. However, the story we heard from the caver who believes that a 'presence' or the feeling of being watched actually saved his life is really interesting for me; it could indicate the presence of sixth-sense powers – which, in my opinion, is just as fascinating as the possibility of ghosts.

Yvette: *This was a really unusual investigation for us; not a house, or a castle, or an ancient ruin, but a geological phenomenon. The history and geography of the place were so absorbing that for a while on my tour I actually forgot we were doing an investigation; but then we asked Gary, our excellent guide, to turn the lights off. It was then that things turned nasty for me. I felt like someone was watching me. You could say – as I'm sure Ciarán will – that my imagination got the better of me, but I've been to lots of scary places in my time and been plunged into total darkness, and I've never had to ask for the lights to be turned back on so fast. Also I had been feeling fine during my trip; I wasn't spooked at all and I was feeling pleasantly warm, but once Gary turned the lights back on I wanted to get out of the caves as fast as possible and my hands were freezing. I can't explain that.*

What the cavers told me was really interesting, especially as they were scientifically minded guys and unlikely to make something like this up. I believe that what they told us they sensed may have been similar to what I felt, although there were noticeable differences between our experiences. Like me, they sensed a presence when they were in here in total darkness, but unlike me they described the presence they felt as benevolent. I'm not sure about what I sensed, but whatever it was

I know it didn't want me or us there. Perhaps it's just people like cavers – who are bravely exploring parts of the earth no one has ever explored before – who are welcome.

Our exploration of the Derbyshire Peaks has been fascinating. I'm so used to doing ghost investigations that this was a refreshing change. Picking up bits of intriguing information here and there about local hauntings, and the different but equally mysterious Black Dogs and sightings of strange lights, was great too. It was almost like we were on a treasure trail, trying to track down anything and everything supernatural.

All in all, the Devil's Arse reminded me of the set for The Lord of the Rings; *you could easily imagine Gollum jumping out from the caves at any moment, mumbling about his 'precious', or shadowy riders following you silently in the darkness. It's a deliciously eerie place and I'd love to take my family there one day for an educational and memorable day out – as long as the tour guide promises to keep the lights on next time!*

6

HEVER CASTLE

A classic haunted castle with a splendid but tragic royal past, the pull of Hever Castle was too powerful for us to resist. The childhood home of Anne Boleyn, the leading lady in one of England's most famous, romantic, but ultimately terrible real-life stories, Hever must have some intrigues in store for the enthusiastic ghost hunter.

THE HISTORY OF HEVER

Hever Castle has grown over the centuries, from its thirteenth-century beginnings as a lowly farmhouse to a fortified manor house and, in the fifteenth century, into its current castle form. After its spell as the Boleyn family home in the sixteenth century it later became the property of another of Henry VIII's unfortunate wives, Anne of Cleves. Its ownership then passed to the Waldegrave family and subsequently to the Meade-Waldos, before it was bought by the American millionaire William Waldorf Astor, who restored it to its former glory. It is now used as a conference centre and is open to the public. Part of its popularity must be due to its rich, turbulent, and wonderfully dramatic and colourful past.

The land on which Hever stands was a gift from William the Conqueror to a Norman noble called Walter de Hevere (d'Evere) in 1066, and subsequently the farmhouse that had stood there was converted, first into a more imposing manor house, before being further developed into the castle with moat that we still know today.

By 1459 Sir Geoffrey Bullen of Norfolk, then Lord Mayor of London, took possession of the castle. The spelling of the family name was different then, but he was in fact the first Boleyn to own it. The castle was passed down through the family and came into the possession of Anne's father Thomas Bullen in 1505.

The date of Anne's birth is disputed (best estimates seem to be either 1501 or 1507), so it is not clear whether the family owned the castle at the time of her birth or if she moved there as a young girl. Hever remained under Boleyn ownership throughout Henry VIII's courtship of Anne (he is known to have visited the castle), their subsequent marriage, and her trial and execution. In 1539 Henry VIII took back ownership of the castle, and found a use for it in 1540 when he divorced Anne of Cleves and granted it to her to live in, effectively banishing her to the place. By 1557 the castle was in Catholic hands; it was given to Sir Edward Waldegrave, notoriously fervent in his faith, by the then Queen, Mary, whose actions in support of her Catholic beliefs earned her the nickname Bloody Mary.

By 1561 Sir Edward's fortunes had changed again and, with the country now under the Protestant rule of Mary's sister Queen Elizabeth, he was found guilty of celebrating the Catholic Mass in secret and plotting against the Queen, and ended his days in the Tower of London. At this point a secret room, shielded from prying eyes by panelling, was added to the castle, probably for hiding Catholic priests from the Queen's soldiers.

The secret room was probably also used to hide dissidents, of the political kind this time, in the turbulent days of Royalists pitting themselves against Parliamentarians in the mid-1600s. At this point the castle was owned by fervent Royalists.

From 1684 onwards Hever was owned by one Henry Waldegrave, 1st Baron, who was an accountant in King James II's household and, more sensationally, husband to the King's illegitimate daughter Henrietta FitzJames.

In the middle of the eighteenth century the castle was bought by a major local landowning family, the Meade-Waldos. It then gradually fell into disrepair until in 1903 it was purchased by William Waldorf Astor, who restored it extensively; his creations included the lake and gardens, and a Tudor-style village, which he used as guest accommodation. Since 1983 Hever Castle has been owned by a company called Broadland Properties Ltd, who have opened it to the public.

Quite a history! Dissidence both religious and political, not to mention sad stories such as that of Anne of Cleves, shunned by Henry VIII, and the persistent whiff of scandal and disrepute, seem to have surrounded Hever down the centuries. Even without the presence of Anne Boleyn, Hever would surely exert a serious pull on the imagination. Anne's story, though, is of course particularly compelling. It should come as no surprise, when the facts of her vivid and ultimately tragic life are known, that the ghost that is most often reportedly seen at Hever is hers.

THE STORY OF ANNE BOLEYN

Born at the very beginning of the sixteenth century, Anne Boleyn was the middle child of Thomas Boleyn or Bullen, Earl of Ormonde (an earldom with roots in Ireland) and Elizabeth Boleyn, formerly Elizabeth Howard, daughter of the Duke of Norfolk. At the age of only eleven Anne was sent to the Netherlands to be educated. There is great speculation as to why she was sent away at such a young age. One theory is that, by contrast with her sister Mary, who was beautiful and desirable by the standards of the time, with blonde hair and pale colouring, Anne had dark eyes and hair, and dark, olive skin. With such an unconventional-looking daughter, perhaps her parents felt that an exceptional education would give her an advantage over other women that she did not have by virtue of her looks alone.

Anne's education in the Netherlands was similar to the modern 'finishing school' experience. She learned about the arts and how to dance; she was taught philosophy, French and how to be a good lady-in-waiting. After acquiring these skills, essential for high-born ladies of the day, the teenage Anne was sent to France to work as a lady-in-waiting to Queen Claude.

She returned to England, on her father's orders, around 1522, and soon after her arrival Henry VIII's eyes fell upon her. Henry was determined, even ruthless, in his efforts to win Anne. She steadfastly refused to be his mistress, however, rejecting all his gifts and advances, which only seemed to spur him on. At one point Henry made her Marchioness of Pembroke, giving her a brooch engraved with the words 'Do not touch me for I am Caesar's'. Together with Henry's persistent advances, Anne's increasingly high public profile meant that she was gradually becoming a celebrity, the talk of the court and of the general public.

Anne eventually gave in to Henry's advances. On the night their union was consummated, it is said, Anne wore a nightgown so tiny and flimsy that you could pass it through a ring! The two were still not married; Henry was still married to Catherine of

Aragon and divorce was not permitted under the Catholic law of the time. To escape his marriage to Catherine (who was deeply loyal to her Catholic faith) and clear his way to marrying Anne, Henry needed to break away from the rule of the Pope and the Vatican, and he did so. He found justification in the Bible for his claim that his marriage to Catherine was cursed by God, to enable himself to divorce her, and declared himself the supreme head of the Church of England and beyond the reach of the Catholic Church. Henry's actions caused seismic upheaval; years of civil unrest, war, and the bloody persecution of both Catholics and Protestants were to follow.

England Needs a Prince

When Anne retired to Greenwich Palace on 6 September 1533 for the birth of her first child, the whole country, Henry included, waited with bated breath, although of course for different reasons. Perhaps Catholics wished for the child not to live, while Protestants may have imagined a Protestant heir to carry on their cause of reforming the country's religion. Already the father of a daughter, Mary, Henry now desperately needed a male heir to ensure the continuance of his line. Under this intense scrutiny, some time between 3 and 4 p.m. on 7 September, Anne gave birth to a baby girl. She is said to have held the baby princess aloft and said, 'We are young, there will be more.'

In fact Anne was not to give birth to any more children, although she went through at least three miscarriages in her attempts to give Henry the prince he so wanted. Of course, ironically enough, Anne's one surviving child would go on to rule England as Queen Elizabeth I, perhaps the greatest of England's royal rulers, but at the time Henry, incensed by the continuing lack of a male heir and probably frightened about the implications for his bloodline, began the machinations for the removal of Anne and the installation of Jane Seymour as his new queen.

Members of Anne's circle, previously the glittering 'celebrities' of Henry's court, were imprisoned and in many cases tortured. Vicious torture eventually forced out of Mark Smeaton, a court musician and friend of Anne's, an almost certainly false confession to an adulterous affair with the Queen. Anne's sister-in-law Jane Parker gave evidence that Anne had indulged in incest with her own brother. Years later, as Jane was about to be executed herself for her part in another scandal at Henry's court, she was to admit that she had lied. Coupled with these claims of adultery and incest were accusations of witchcraft. There had always been an element of disbelief in court and amongst the public that the king could be so in love with a woman who was so 'unattractive' – at least by the conventions of the day.

Anne's looks, the confessions of those under torture or with motivations of their own, and her continuing failure to produce Henry's desperately wished-for male child, all conspired against her and the woman previously fêted and adored as Queen of England found herself awaiting her fate in the notorious Tower of London.

Up to her last moments, Anne said nothing against Henry, referring to him always as 'My noble King.' Even on the very day of her execution in May 1536, she reportedly kept glancing over her shoulder, hoping for a last-minute reprieve. In an act of 'mercy', Henry had had brought over from France a specially trained swords-man to perform the beheading with the sharpest possible blade, to give Anne a swifter death than that granted by the usual axe. There was complete silence apart from an ominous drum roll as the executioner flourished his French blade. Anne reacted to a shout from the crowd by turning her head in the direction of the sound. It was then that the executioner swung his sword.

Anne's Restless Ghost

Oh Death
Rock me asleep
Bring on my quiet rest
Let pass my very guiltless ghost
Out of my careful breast
Ring out the doleful knell
Let it sound
My death tell
For I must die.

ATTRIBUTED TO ANNE BOLEYN

Anne wrote longingly of her 'quiet rest' in death, but arguably she has not found it. Ever since her death numerous hauntings have been attributed to the executed queen. As well as being seen at Hever Castle, her apparition has been reported at another of her family's homes, Blickling Hall in Norfolk. She is also said to appear sometimes at the Tower of London, the grim palace-prison where she spent her last days and met her end. Here her ghost is said to wander Tower Green and the Chapel Royal. In addition, eyewitness reports have her wandering the grounds of Rochford Hall in Essex, a one-time home of her family. In these sightings Anne is said to be headless, although in other locations she appears as she would have in life, sometimes walking across the grounds, sometimes in a horse-drawn carriage.

At Hever, our destination in our search for Anne's ghost, she is said to appear every Christmas Eve, walking over the River Eden bridge in the castle grounds. Her ghost is also often reportedly seen standing under the great oak tree where Henry originally courted her. It seems that even in death, Anne Boleyn cannot find peace.

Ada Meade-Waldo, whose husband, Viscount Astor Waldo, owned Hever Castle in the 1890s, believed firmly in the presence of Anne Boleyn's ghost at the castle. Ada would complain that whenever she visited Hever (it was not the family's main home), Anne made it unpleasant for her. She was also quite convinced that she had actually met Anne one Boxing Day. Her husband also had an interest in the occult; in fact, the history of Hever and the legend of Anne's ghost was said to have been one of the factors that attracted him to the castle. What is known for sure is that after he had restored the house, he engaged the Society for Psychical Research to hold watch in the castle over several Christmases. Unfortunately on those occasions Anne did not put in an appearance.

Yvette: *Ever since I was a little girl I've wanted to wear those long dresses that queens and princesses wore in the movies. I was intrigued by history books that had pictures of Henry VIII and I was even more interested in reading about his wives. As I got older I often wondered what woman in their right mind would marry a man who chopped off your head if he was displeased with you. I bought many books on the subject and would often sit for hours looking at the paintings and pictures of Henry, his famous wives and of the beautiful palaces that they occupied. My curiosity for and love of the Tudor period means that my house looks like the inside of a museum and if I could wear long, flowing, corseted dresses without looking completely ridiculous then I would.*

The house that Karl and I bought four years ago dates back to Tudor times, and we have made sure that the furniture is in keeping with the style of the house. So now I have my own little palace. I'll just have to remember to behave myself otherwise Karl may want to chop my head off!

So I think you'll have realised by now what a huge fan I am of anything to do with the Tudor period. You can imagine my delight and excitement then when Ciarán told me we were off to investigate Hever Castle, the childhood home of Anne Boleyn. I was behaving like a child on Christmas Eve on the night of the investigation. We would be spending the night, just the two of us, in the castle. At first I couldn't believe our luck and couldn't wait to get going – just the thought of walking amongst the family's personal things, to be able to go into Anne Boleyn's bedchamber and to walk down the corridors that she or Henry would have walked, filled me with sheer delight. But all that changed when I saw the castle for the first time in the dark. All of a sudden I felt a little nervous. I soon discovered there was good reason to be nervous, as you will see from our account of spending the night at Hever Castle.

Hever Castle is a huge building with many rooms, which makes it very difficult to cover fully with just the two of us. The key to investigating an allegedly haunted location is to focus the investigation on areas where previous eyewitnesses have reported phenomena. To find out where the ghostly activity at Hever is most concentrated, we gathered accounts from staff, eyewitnesses, historical accounts and prior investigations. Here's what we found.

THE CASE OF HEVER CASTLE

A few years ago a visitor and her daughter were in the room known as the Henry VIII bedroom when the girl asked, 'Who is that horrible-looking man sitting there?' The mother could only see an empty chair, but the child insisted that there was a large man sitting in the corner of the room staring directly at them. A couple of years later a student visiting the castle saw this 'horrible-looking man' too. Although we couldn't find any written proof that this would have been Henry's bedroom, it is certainly the largest bedroom in the building, which suggests that Henry could well have been its occupant.

The section of the castle containing the relatively recently added Morning Room was, back in the thirteenth century, a gatehouse. The old staircase from the gatehouse, situated now in the far-right corner of the Morning Room, is said to be haunted by the ghost of a priest. A researcher, part of a film crew, once came running away from the room insisting that there was 'something evil' up the stairs. The background of this area certainly suggests that it is ripe for haunting; there is a secret room there that was probably used as a 'priest hole'.

What was a priest hole? During the persecution of England's Catholics in Queen Elizabeth's day, many secret hideouts were made in pro-Catholic houses to hide away Catholic priests from the investigations of the Queen's men. The priest hole at Hever is tiny and airless; no one could have survived there for long. It is not too fanciful to imagine some unfortunate priest, trapped too long in that little room waiting for Elizabeth's men to finish searching the house, suffocating and eventually being found dead. The lingering spirit of an unfortunate priest, torn between fear of asphyxiation and dread of the Queen's men, may well be what gives this part of the castle its air of dread and gloom.

In the Long Gallery is a plinth on a windowsill. A few years ago a guide in the gallery heard a loud bang, and looked round to see the plinth lying on the floor. The guide was alone in the room at the time. The sighting of a mysterious ghostly man on a horse has also been reported in there. The gallery is said by many to be the 'nastiest' part of the castle, and people often report feeling inexplicably ill in this part of the building. The oldest part of the castle, and the place where the priest hole would have been ... is it surprising that the staff say that they don't like being in there or going down the gallery's stairs on their own?

The ghost of Anne Boleyn is popularly said to walk the grounds of the castle, seeming to especially favour Boxing Day. And in recent times a member of staff saw in the grounds a man in jousting costume. The staff member assumed that he was a casual worker, there for one of the castle's frequent medieval-themed events. Later on they discovered that there was no

such event happening on that day. Could the unidentified man have been a ghost?

In the Staircase Gallery, people often report feeling
as though someone is touching their hair. Tour guides
have also heard footsteps and the rustle of skirts, but
been unable to find anyone when they investigated.
Visitors have often said that they feel the strange
sensation that the staircase is falling away from them
as they go up it, almost as if the present is dissolving
into the past and they are about to 'slip' through
time itself.

Given the wealth of reported paranormal activity that
we uncovered, and the size of Hever Castle, ideally
we would want to investigate and monitor the castle
for at least a year and to have investigation teams
working in every single room and area where activity
has been reported. Unfortunately that just isn't
practical, so we decided to focus on the areas that
interested us the most: the grounds, the Long Gallery,
Anne Boleyn's room and the Staircase Gallery.

Our Investigation Begins

We are both tingling with excitement as we enter
Hever's grounds. It is a castle straight out of a childhood fairytale. Ivy creeps up the front wall, suffocating
the stone above the drawbridge, threatening to enter
via the front windows. We can't help wondering

whether there are other, more ethereal foes trying to get into or out of the place!

We explore the grounds first in the fading light. The castle's magnificent gardens and grounds include the Italian Garden, filled with statuary and sculpture from Roman and Renaissance times; a maze; a vast, sparkling lake, and a rose garden. It's difficult to imagine what the castle grounds would have looked like in Anne's time – and they certainly didn't include the twentieth-century Yew Maze or the Adventure Playground! – but, despite all this modernisation, Anne's ghost has been spotted in the grounds approximately fifteen times since her death; an average of three sightings a century.

It is almost completely dark as we decide to head into the castle; the atmosphere feels dense and heavy and the bushes and trees rustle gently as we pass them. If it wasn't for the sound of planes overhead, which destroys a little of the magic, we could almost feel as if we have been transported back in time.

We cross over the drawbridge, looking at the some-how comforting and welcoming light reflecting on the moat. We both feel incredibly privileged to be in this magnificent place. As we step inside we think about the many well-known figures from the past who must have walked exactly this route.

Once inside we can scarcely contain our excitement at being in the house where Anne Boleyn was born. Neither of us are frightened; we are too excited to be afraid. The inside of the castle is smaller than we expected, but this doesn't take away from its beauty.

We switch our night-vision cameras on and flick on our torches – it's very dark in here – and start to explore. As we walk through this first section, the Inner Hall, which is full of Tudor décor and furniture, we admire the portraits that adorn the walls. A Holbein painting of Anne Boleyn grabs our attention and we silently wonder if she will show herself tonight.

The grand dining hall really reflects the grandeur of Anne's time, with its magnificent tapestries and huge, imposing fireplace. We take a moment there to plan our next move. Ciarán is very keen to position some temperature data loggers in this area as he's wondering if the reports of temperature drops at the castle may be explicable by the enormous and probably draughty fireplace.

Ciarán: *Temperature drops have long been associated with haunting experiences – 'cold spots' are said to be linked with the presence of spirit. This is certainly the case with some of the reports from Hever Castle. However, it's worth bearing in mind that the correlation between hauntings and temperature is made much of by the media and therefore possibly already in the fore-front of someone's mind. Television programmes, including our own* Most Haunted, *tend to portray a person's detection of a ghostly presence as a drop in temperature. Perhaps someone in a supposedly haunted*

location, on feeling a perfectly explicable drop in temper-
ature, might be influenced by this to assume that it
means a ghost is present? My research, however, has
revealed that this is not exclusively a contemporary
phenomenon. There are accounts going back over a
hundred years of cold breezes, chilling 'presences' and
temperature drops. In 1925, for example, the ghost-
hunter and researcher Harry Price recorded temperature
drops during his experiments with the medium Stella
C., while she was in contact with spirit.

Back in the present, here in Hever Castle I'm partic-
ularly conscious of the structure of the place and how
there are some very obvious channels for air, like the
fireplace. I'm going to place several temperature data
loggers around the room and also a few in adjoining
rooms, to compare and contrast the temperatures.

Both of us would love to study the portraits and
artefacts for longer – everything here is fascinating –
but we are aware that we haven't got permission to
be in the castle alone for long and no paranormal
activity has been reported in these rooms. We move
quickly through the library and then find ourselves
standing in front of the priest hole.

Yvette: *This is wild, wicked, amazing. I cannot believe*
I am here. It's a dream come true for me to be in this
place. I'm a huge fan of Tudor history; the corsets, the
drama, everything about that period fascinates me. So

far I haven't sensed anything paranormal or unusual but that could be because I feel so excited. We are standing outside the priest hole now where I know a priest may have suffocated and died, and it's having a dampening effect on my spirits. Such a horrible way to die! I'm going to call out to see if his spirit is still lingering here. Did you hear that, Ciarán? I heard a faint knocking sound. There it is again.

Ciarán: *Yvette has just told me she heard a faint knocking sound twice but I can't hear anything; although a few minutes ago I did think I heard a voice – it sounded like a child or a baby crying. Then again it could have been the echo of my voice or Yvette's in the doorway. Like Yvette I'm finding it hard to concentrate on the investigation here. The history of the place is making my mind race and I can't keep my mind clear because all the movies I've seen about the period and memories of my school history lessons are flooding back to me. I feel so honoured and privileged to be here.*

Anne Boleyn's Bedroom

Incredible! We are walking up the same stairs that Anne Boleyn would have walked many times on her way to her bedroom. The markings on the wall look so intricate. Here we are!

As soon as we step inside, any sense of awe we experienced is somewhat diminished as we find ourselves ducking to avoid hitting our heads on the low doorways. The grand public rooms at Hever are breathtaking, but impressive public areas in Tudor times often came at the expense of the private rooms – especially the private room of a mere daughter. As a result, Anne's bedroom is very cramped and small. It has some fascinating features though; the half-domed ceiling and the huge pieces of furniture that dominate the room. It also has pretty lattice windows recessed into the walls to form the back of a window seat. Perhaps Anne used to sit in that seat.

The room is so small that our torches light it up easily and thoroughly. There are several pictures of Anne and, in one corner, the book of hours that she gave to her friend and kinswoman Margaret Lee moments before her beheading, asking her to pass to Sir Thomas Wyatt. Knowing how Anne would have treasured that book, seeing it with our own eyes makes us both shiver as if touched by a ghost.

The room feels too cramped and small to call out and neither of us are feeling anything strange, just excitement at being in Anne Boleyn's room, so we decide to head down to the infamous Long Gallery.

The Long Gallery and Staircase

We are walking down a corridor towards the Long Gallery and Yvette doesn't like it all. Even though we have just been in Anne's tiny room, Yvette says she feels more claustrophobic out here than she did up there. There are mannequins lined up along the gallery, dressed in period costume, and there is a strong sense that one of them could jump out at us at any moment.

Yvette: *I can't describe it but if feels as if all my worst nightmares are about to come true. I'm experiencing a sense of absolute and inexplicable dread. I didn't feel anything but excitement in Anne's room but this is a different story. I feel as if something horrible is about to happen. This is awful. If this is in any way related to a feeling of precognition, I don't want it. I feel like we are being followed and I want to run. I don't want to go on any more. I'm feeling shaky. I also think I heard a bang from the far end of the gallery even though there's absolutely nobody there. It would take us about ten minutes to run to another part of the castle to where the staff are. It was a loud bang and I hope it's not a sign that something is coming our way. I wasn't expecting this, Ciarán, I'm scared, really scared!*

Ciarán: *It's very quiet and dark in here and Yvette has started to panic a bit, which I don't understand as until now she has been so happy and excited. I must admit I'm feeling a bit apprehensive too but I'm not sure if that's because I'm being influenced by Yvette's fear or by the dummies in costume we are walking past. I know the ghost of a horse has been seen here too and I do get the feeling that something might jump out at me any moment. I'm very conscious of time as we only have very limited time here. It's not right to end the investigation at this point with us feeling the way we are and also considering we've just heard a bang. I feel as though we should stay at least another fifteen minutes to see what develops and to truly investigate the noise. I'm secretly hoping it happens again but I think Yvette will be pleased to leave this area fairly soon!*

We stay in the Long Gallery for another half an hour, calling out and filming every inch of the room, hoping to capture some more auditory phenomena on the microphones, but everything is very quiet. We walk down to the end and investigate the exhibition room, wondering if the banging sound came from there. Neither of us really wants to leave as we don't feel we have spent nearly enough time here, but sadly it is time to go. Ciarán quickly rounds up his temperature data loggers, and takes captures of the ambient temperature and air movement in the dining room and surrounding rooms using his thermal imager. We decide to leave via the gatehouse with its grisly collection of torture instruments, and then head back outside to the grounds. Before walking to our car we both take one last look at the huge oak tree and imagine Anne there, laughing and very much in love with her future husband, King Henry VIII.

Conclusion

Yvette: *For me this is by far the most exciting location I've visited for the book. It's the history of the place that's got me; who knows, perhaps in a past life I lived in that era! I don't know what it is but something about the Tudor period pulls me towards it. For this reason I must be the worst person to do an investigation here as my mind is too filled with images from films, books and documentaries about the Tudors and especially Henry VIII and Anne Boleyn. I didn't sense her unhappy presence here – in fact in her room I felt very content – but I did sense something vile in the Long Gallery. I was convinced something was about to jump out and grab me, which, curiously, is something visitors have reported here before. I also hated the gatehouse, the last room we visited, but this wasn't for any paranormal reasons but because it contains those horrible torture instruments, including beheading axes.*

Ciarán: *It was hard for us to do an impartial investigation at Hever as we are both so heavily influenced by our knowledge of the events that have taken place here and the famous historical figures who have lived at the castle. I didn't think this would have had quite such an effect on our investigation, but it did. Our sense of excitement also probably spoiled things – it made it hard for us to really listen and observe because our minds were racing with ideas and images. What makes the investigation stand out for me, however, was Yvette's sense of dread – which I may have picked up on too – in the Long Gallery, as that is something people have reported numerous times. The problem is that there are cues in the form of those mannequins, which could ignite that sense of dread or anticipation. I know I've been similarly spooked at an investigation of Warwick Castle when I was surrounded by mannequins. The temperature data didn't reveal any anomalies and there is a slight drop the closer you get to the fireplace. The thermal imager did reveal a slight cool air movement coming from there. I'm truly honoured to have been allowed into the castle alone and I'm sure, in daylight, it takes on a whole different feel.*

As we drive away from the castle, Yvette again expresses her disappointment at not seeing Anne's ghost. Perhaps, though, her feeling of contentment in Anne's room was the appropriate reaction. Maybe it was Anne's benign influence. Yvette's apprehension in the Long Gallery could have been to do with the spirit of a priest from the past, doomed to die in the tiny hidden room there. Similarly the bang heard could have been to do with the priest's attempts to escape, or it could simply have been a temperature drop affecting the wood. Either way, Hever Castle had some truly strange and creepy moments that simply beg for further investigation. A place with a fascinating history and, perhaps, fascinating spirits.

PART TWO:

And Abroad

Compared to the UK and USA, where it sometimes seems that almost anybody you talk to has either had a paranormal experience or knows a story of someone who has, the French seem to be somewhat more guarded about discussing such experiences or even taking the topic very seriously. This is, again, reflected in the country's media. In contemporary France there are hardly any TV programmes dealing with the paranormal, and what drama series there have been on the subject have focused less on hauntings and more on phenomena such as precognition and telepathy. Historically, though, France does have a background in the paranormal and some famous names in the fields of paranormal research and parapsychology have a connection with the country.

The Paranormal in France

Active interest in the paranormal in France reached a peak with the development of the social movement of Spiritism in the mid-nineteenth century. Academically, the founding of the IMI (Institut Métapsychique International) in 1919 was a milestone. Essentially a research institute devoted to parapsychology topics, it boasted such famous figures of the time as the Nobel Prize-winning scientist Charles Richet and the celebrated astronomer Camille Flammarion.

And what about today? A 2002 survey by a French researcher at Dublin City University compared and contrasted paranormal belief in the UK, France, and the USA. According to the results, the French have a stronger belief in precognition and telepathy, as well as in astrology, while people in the UK and USA believe much more in ghosts and after-death communication. Over fifty per cent of respondents in those two countries said they believed in ghosts, compared to just eleven per cent in France.

A personal experience that Ciarán had in Paris slightly contradicts these findings, though, and suggests that public interest may be stronger than the survey results indicate. On a visit to the famous Père Lachaise Cemetery in Paris, where luminaries from Chopin to Oscar Wilde and Edith Piaf are buried, he approached the grave of Allan Kardec, the founder of Spiritism.

Ciarán: *I walked up to Kardec's grave and was taken aback by the constant stream of visitors. There wasn't a queue but I had to wait at least half an hour as people paying their respects or leaving flowers came and went, before I could look closely at the grave uninterrupted. Then, as I was walking away, a woman arrived with a bunch of flowers, laid them down, touched the gravestone, bowed her head and muttered a few words before leaving. It was an ordinary lunchtime, mid-week, and was not a special anniversary of Kardec or Spiritism.*

The mixed messages in all this intrigued us. Do people in France have less belief in ghosts than, say, Americans? If so, why such reverence and so many people at Allan Kardec's grave? And if there *is* less belief in ghosts, why? Are there actually fewer ghosts in France for people to see? And if so, why would they have a geographical preference and appear more in the UK and the USA than across the Channel? There was a lot to think about here, but the one thing we were sure of was that we wanted to go and find out more for ourselves. So we packed our bags and headed over to France to spend a few weeks investigating haunting phenomena, and to see whether ghosts really are less common there than here at home. As you will learn as you read on, we really had no idea what were letting ourselves in for . . .

1

CHÂTEAU DU PAYS LAURAGAIS

It's the summer of 2006 and we are about to start our investigations in a small village in the Pays Lauragais or Lauragais country, located south of Toulouse in the south-west of France. The village is quite famous locally for its recently restored windmill, but what we are really interested in is the paranormal activity that has been reported at the deserted château that sits at the outskirts of the village. It is a small and very quiet place, and for that reason we wished to protect the privacy of the villagers and keep the location secret by giving the château and some of the individuals who agreed to share their stories pseudonyms.

THE CASE OF THE CHÂTEAU: MURDER, SUICIDE AND FOUL PLAY

The stories in circulation about the Château du Pays Lauragais all have dark and sinister associations. For starters, it seems that one of its owners may have been involved in arson and murder. Information on these events is limited, but we have been able to gather from local sources that there are long-running rumours and stories about the château being abandoned and deliberately ruined to cover up a malicious crime committed in the early twentieth century. Some of these accounts are particularly florid, and they tend to take on embellishments and change their key facts regularly depending on who you're talking to. The exact nature of the crime is therefore impossible to pin down, but stories vary from the tale of a pregnant woman being killed because the child was unwanted, to the theory that an employee was silenced for ever because the unfortunate individual discovered illegal financial dealings by the master of the castle. This is all very murky, and difficult to verify, but there are two stories surrounding the château that are incontestably true; one concerns a teenage girl who committed suicide in the interior in the late nineties.

The precise location of the suicide is unknown, but after persistent prodding we learn from some local residents that they believe she hung herself above the stairwell. No one has reported seeing the girl's ghost, but the uneasy feeling people say they experience when visiting the château could well be related to some residual presence caused by the traumatic event.

Residual Hauntings

Residual hauntings are thought to be sensory replays of previous events in a building. These replays can manifest as sounds, like footsteps, voices or music. They can also be figures walking across a room then suddenly vanishing, or scenes involving a number of people (e.g. a dinner in a castle or a fight between two men). With visual phenomena, eyewitnesses will automatically assume that they have seen a ghost. The fundamental difference, though, appears to be that there is no interaction with the figures seen – interaction is in fact impossible – and that the same activity is played out time and time again. Residual hauntings, therefore, don't actually involve spirits in the traditional sense of the word.

Ciarán does not favour the term 'residual' and prefers to refer to this phenomenon as the 'Stone Tape Theory.' This refers to the theory that energy becomes imprinted on the stone, the fabric that makes up buildings. The stones in the walls 'play back' the movements and emotions of those who once lived there. People like mediums and psychics are sometimes able to sense or even interact with these energies. The imprinted energy can also be picked up by people like Yvette who are not mediums but who are highly sensitive.

One of the key ideas behind Stone Tape Theory is that, just as an iron remains hot long after it's turned off, strong energy in other forms can be retained by physical surroundings. Yvette's feeling is that absolutely everything in the universe is made of energy, which, according to a basic law of physics, can be changed but cannot be destroyed. Ciarán is not so sure of applying this idea to hauntings, suggesting that it is probably 'pseudoscience'. Yvette is sticking firmly to her theory though, and she also suggests that when someone witnesses this kind of haunting and is startled or frightened by it, the energy from their emotions in turn may 'recharge' the environment so that the manifestations keep happening. And so it goes on.

Back to our research into the château, and we are fast discovering that the locals don't like talking about the place. The few who can be persuaded mutter words like 'evil' or 'foul play'. One man who heard footsteps in the stairwell told Ciarán that he was so terrified he has not returned to the château in the ten years since it happened, even though he lives nearby. He has quite a story to tell:

```
I have never liked the place. Sometimes
I even try to find an alternative route
past it. There are friends of mine who
feel the same way and sometimes we joke
about it, saying, you know, it was just
because we were kids and messed about,
and used to tell ghost stories about
the place. I think there's more to it.
```

A couple of incidents have stuck in my mind.

The first time something happened that wasn't necessarily ghostly, but it was weird. We were playing paintball in the forest and fields around the château. You weren't meant to, but we were young so we didn't care! After we'd been there for an hour or so we saw torches through the trees, and shouting and dogs barking, so we all crouched down and kept quiet. Eventually the torches and voices came closer and we realised it was the police, so we stood up and showed ourselves. The police questioned us about the night before, wanting to know if we'd been in the forest playing and if we'd played in the château last night. It turned out that a young girl had hung herself there that night, by standing on a chair and pushing it away. We answered 'no' to the barrage of questions because we didn't want to get in trouble, but in fact we had been playing in the forest the night before, and some of us had heard some eerie screeching sounds and a thump. We had put it down to night animals, you know, an owl catching a mouse or something

like that. It had still frightened us
enough that we finished the game early.
To think, we were there when she committed suicide and we had no idea . . .

One evening a few months later we were
playing inside the château, trying to
scare a friend of mine who'd never been
there before. I'd run upstairs ready to
scare him but then realised he was still
downstairs. I ran down and jumped out
from behind a wall. We nearly wet
ourselves at his screaming. We had to
stop him from running away! When we had
calmed down we went upstairs again, but
at the top of the stairs I froze. A
single chair was in the middle of the
floor right by the top of the stairs. I
was the only one who had been up there
that evening until that point, and when
I was there the chair had definitely
been off to the side. If it'd been in
the middle like that I would have fallen
over it or had to move it when I ran
downstairs to scare my friend. I tried
to convince my friends but they just
laughed, thinking I was still playing
jokes. We also, on other occasions,
heard footsteps and noises coming from
upstairs, all over the place but mostly

```
in the area of the stairs. I've had
other friends who've said they've heard
the thump of the chair falling upstairs,
gone to investigate and the chair is
just sitting there by a window . . .
Place still creeps me out just talking
about it.'
```

The same eyewitness mentioned a story, that we'd heard a bit about, of the ghost of the lady who died at the château in horrible and sad circumstances. He says he has never seen it but has heard accounts from some of the older locals. Apparently the ghost of the lady is visible on a clear night, and usually when the moon is full, standing at one of the château's upper windows.

The history behind the apparition is that in the early 1900s the local count, who then lived in the château, was getting married and was waiting inside for his bride. She was approaching the château down the country lane leading to it, thrilled at the prospect of the day about to unfold before her. As she turned a corner, however, a charging horse and carriage came upon her, killing her instantly and gruesomely. Could this, rather than the story of the covered-up crime, be the truth behind the haunting of the Château du Pays Lauragais? It is certainly historically accurate; we have heard corroborating accounts of the events from other locals, and there is reference to the wedding and the tragic accident in historical documents.

We also heard a strange story from another man who recalled playing around the château as a young adult. His experience seems, chillingly, to tie in with the bride's tragic accident.

```
I always went there with two friends,
on motorbikes. When we went as
teenagers we only had little bikes but
as we got older the bikes got more
powerful. No matter what bike this one
guy was on, though, it always broke
down. We visited the château a handful
of times and every time we tried to
leave his motorbike wouldn't start. A
couple of times he had even borrowed
his brother's brand-new bike, but each
time they got to the same point on the
lane and the bike just died. We've
since learned that it was at that point
in the lane where the lady was killed.
```

We couldn't wait to get started on our investigation, but as you will see, we soon came to understand why the locals give the château such a wide berth ...

Our Investigation Begins
As we drive to our destination, we admire the stunning countryside undulating away into the distance, and chat about France and its rich, wonderful history of

mysteries and legends. It's so exciting for us both to be here and to be carrying out our first European mainland investigation. We pass the signpost announcing that we have reached the village, and drive slowly through it, weaving our way along the deserted streets and past a tranquil town hall and serene church. It certainly does feel like a ghost town.

The château is situated just outside the village, and we stop briefly on the brow of a hill to take in an undisturbed view of it. It sits, looking deceptively peaceful, nestled amongst acres of dry grassland and gentle hills. It's set about 200 yards from the road, surrounded by signs warning 'propriété privée' and 'défense d'entrer'. We doubt that any potential trespassers would need these signs to keep them away, though. If there was a vote for 'location most likely to be haunted', this would surely be a winner! Imagine if you will a two-storey mansion, several hundred years old, abandoned and completely deserted, standing desolate in the middle of nowhere. Now imagine that the building is run-down, blackened, and practically gutted, seemingly by fire, so that only fragments of its original finery and splendour remain. We look at each other and at exactly the same time smile and say out loud, 'Blair Witch Project.'

A little while later, when we begin our investigation proper, we don't feel much like smiling any more. The light is fading and the château's looming presence in the distance is proving strangely unsettling. But the investigation has to go on, and so, armed with a torch, a compass watch, our cameras and some water, we park the car by the two wooden posts that mark the entrance to the château. We need a compass because although we can easily see the building at the moment, the darkness is falling fast and by nightfall it will be impossible to find our way back without one. We are both looking forward to the investigation, but are also a little apprehensive because we are, after all, in the middle of nowhere. The roads are quiet, there isn't a local in sight, and it is getting darker and darker by the minute. But we know we have taken every possible precaution; we have permission to visit, we have our mobiles in case of emergency, and friends and family know exactly where we are. To give ourselves an energy boost as we begin our climb towards the château, we remind ourselves that we are ghost hunters and this is what we love to do.

Yvette: *The château looks run-down and decayed. We're in the middle of nowhere. Ciarán does pick them! I'm worried that we might get lost. I'm glad I'm wearing my walking boots – this isn't an easy climb. I'm not sure if my heart is beating so fast because of the exercise or because I'm scared. I know nothing about this place and I don't want to know either until after we've had a look around. Ciarán has been here before and knows a little more, but he isn't going to tell me until we finish, as it's important for me to have an open mind. I don't* want to be influenced by anything. We're getting closer now. God it looks even more ominous close up. It also looks a lot bigger. In fact it's huge. Oh my God, there are bats! I should have known there would be, but it's still freaking me out. There's also quite a bit of litter, so obviously it's a place where tramps or partying teenagers hang out. I hope a drunken tramp doesn't suddenly lunge at us in the darkness. At this point I'm more worried about the living than the dead.

Ciarán: I've tried to calm Yvette's concern that there might be tramps or drunks hanging out here by telling her how unlikely it is that they would be here at this time of night and by reminding her of how low the crime rate is in this area of France. I can tell though that Yvette is nervous about more than the odd tramp. I must confess I feel a little nervous too, but then I know the history of the place and my knowledge of what has allegedly happened here may be affecting me. My heart is beating really loudly and the more the light fades the more Gothic and eerie things look. The bats really complete the picture. They are everywhere. I can't see the car any more because the lighting conditions have deteriorated so much. We're going to have to rely one hundred per cent on my compass watch to get us back in one piece. I'm glad that we decided to do this investigation in the summer rather than the winter when weather conditions would just make it impossible. As for the alleged paranormal activity reported here, I've *been told lots of stories but the only thing I've let Yvette know is that I've talked to a few locals and they are convinced that the place is haunted. I can understand why people might think that – it's got all the credentials: an ancient building, deserted, ruined, even occupied by bats, and as night falls it looks like a movie set for your archetypal ghost film. But atmosphere alone isn't enough to convince me that a place is haunted.*

We're standing just outside the main entrance now and for some reason neither of us wants to step inside. Jokingly Yvette reminds me that it's her job to be the one who gets nervous. Yvette thinks she hears a dull thud immediately to her right and the sound of faint moaning, but we agree that the thud may have been a bat and the moan may have been a distant plane, car or motorbike.

Eventually we step inside, and shine our torches around to see what we are letting ourselves in for. Our initial impressions are correct: this really is like the final moments in *The Blair Witch Project*, in which three young student film-makers get lost in the woods while filming a documentary about the eponymous local legend. After being terrorised by an unseen presence for several days, they mysteriously disappear, one by one ... The interior of the château is crumbling and run-down. There is graffiti all over the walls and discarded bottles and cans litter the place. It's also very, very dark and there is a musty smell of decay.

Yvette: *What a find this place is. I was feeling a little sleepy as we drove here this afternoon but I'm wide awake now! I've never felt so alert. It's as if I need to watch my back and I can't afford to relax for one minute. It's not at all easy to walk as the floorboards are broken and we don't want to slip and fall. The stairs also don't look safe, so we won't be climbing those. We would never be able to get a film crew into a place like this; Health and Safety would have a field day. They'd have a point actually. What we are doing today is quite dangerous and I'd feel much happier if we had backup outside. This place really does give me the creeps and I'll be glad when the investigation is over. I'm shining my light above me to look at the ceiling and as I do I think I can hear something creak loudly above me, almost a thump. It's not bats. It sounds like it could be footsteps and they are coming from above the stairwell. I think there's somebody upstairs!*

Ciarán: *Yvette is concerned that there is somebody upstairs, but I know that's not the case as it's impossible to climb the stairs and even if someone did they would break the floorboards and fall through the ceiling. Now that I'm inside the château I feel even more nervous than I did when we were standing outside. I feel something tingling on the back of my neck. It's not my pendant. What is it? My heart is beating so loud I'm surprised Yvette can't hear it. There's that tingling again. It's probably an insect. Yup! I'm right. It's a tiny spider. That's suggestion for you!*

After our initial investigation of the main entrance hall we decide to explore the side rooms. They prove to be equally decayed, run-down and menacing. We decide to call out in both English and French to encourage any spirits to communicate. We use calling out as we always like to have a 'no stone unturned' approach to our work. When we call out we always do so in a sincere, welcoming way, stressing that we mean no harm.

Yvette: *I'm so used to dead silence when I call out that I often assume that is what I'm going to get. It looks like this is no exception. Ciarán's not getting anything either. Or am I being too hasty? I could have sworn I just heard four faint taps. I'm going to call out again. There it is again! I wish they were louder as right now Ciarán can't hear them, only I can, but then women have better hearing than men, don't they? I'll try stone-throwing. I'm going to throw a stone and see if it is thrown back to me. I'm doing this because knocking and tapping sounds are classic signs of haunting. If there's a ghost here he or she might be able to take up the challenge and throw something back at me.*

Ciarán: *Yvette is convinced she heard some faint tapping after we called out. I didn't hear anything but my hearing isn't as sharp as hers. The stone-throwing isn't getting a response, but then again I have never seen this technique work. What's most noticeable for me now is that I feel much more at ease. The initial panic I felt as we approached the building and stepped inside has completely gone. This is because I'm becoming more aware of my surroundings.*

We decide to take a break and go outside for a few minutes. As we walk towards the entrance we both notice something hovering in the window beside the door. At first we dismiss it as a bat, but then we begin to wonder if bats can hover like that?

Outside, the moon is clear and bright but somehow it doesn't seem to illuminate the darkness surrounding the château. Everything is pitch-black and we stumble around for a while trying to get our bearings. We call out again to see if we can pick up any energies outside but the night is quiet; almost too quiet, as we would have expected to hear at least the rustling of bats. In fact we can hear absolutely nothing.

Yvette: *I'm still petrified, but determined to work through this. I'm disappointed that we are not picking up anything but perhaps it's because there are only two of us. There is something about the energy dynamic of a group on a ghost hunt that you can't always reproduce when there are just two of you. One thing I do know is that Ciarán would never have got me to do an investigation in a place as deserted and eerie as this in another country in the middle of nowhere for our first book together. I simply wouldn't have been up to it, especially without my team for backup. It's just too scary. I'm disappointed though that we aren't getting more activity.*

Ciarán: *Yvette is disappointed but I'm going to tell her now that visiting this place is a dream come true for me. That's because one of the phenomena that has been reported here is noises, sometimes footsteps, above the stairwell. Yvette heard that almost as soon as we stepped inside and it was really hard for me to contain my excitement because, without realising it, she was reporting exactly what others have reported before. I think we should go back to the stairwell. I'm feeling uneasy again and I have no idea why.*

We go back to the stairwell where Yvette first heard the 'footsteps' to see if she can hear them again. We stand in silence for at least fifteen minutes, waiting and hoping for an unseen presence, but sadly there is nothing, although at one point Yvette does think she hears a repeat of the faint knocking she heard when she called out. Feeling frustrated, we decide it's time to make our way back to the car.

Yvette: *We're heading back to the car now, which is an adventure in itself! Ciarán is excited about the sounds I heard and it certainly is a coincidence that other people have reported the same experience, but I wanted more. I always want more. Ciarán will fill me in about the history of the place and the phenomena reported here as we drive back. I haven't any idea but I'm convinced that something really nasty, evil even, happened here. It's a very menacing place and I reckon that with a medium here you'd definitely get phenomena. I was absolutely terrified when we arrived and had to work really hard to stay calm and in control because the broken floorboards and the rubble under our feet were very dangerous. It felt as if a trapdoor might open at any moment and swallow us up. I'm glad we've made it back to the car in one piece.*

Ciarán: *I had no idea Yvette was as scared as she is telling me now. I noticed that she was nervous but I'm used to that. Because she didn't grab onto me I assumed she was okay, but now I know she was making a special effort to be brave even though she was so worried about slipping or falling. I'm really proud of her. I think even the most sceptical of ghost hunters couldn't help but feel anxious here. I don't know whether it's the fact that this house is isolated, deserted, run-down or infested with bats, but one thing I do know: spending the night alone here would take a lot of courage, stupidity or whisky! It is the ideal location in terms of suggestion. Without knowing anything about the place, Yvette was already fearful just seeing it for the first time. Yvette is possibly right, it would have been better if we had visited this place with a medium to give the spirits – if there are any here – something to work with. I still remain sceptical of mediums' veracity and accuracy, but what we could do here is bring an English medium in, as they wouldn't have the language to do prior research, or even the time to find out the information it has taken me so long to extract from the locals.*

The sounds Yvette heard in the stairwell make this investigation really stand out for me. Yvette had absolutely no idea that these sounds are the most signif-icant phenomenon here and have been consistently reported by witnesses over a long period of time. As investigators, one of the key things is getting identical independent accounts, and that's what we have with Yvette's experiences together with some of the local testi-monies. Thinking about it with a sceptical head I would have to say that perhaps the dilapidated nature of the château has been the cause of its ghostly reputation. We did see bats and it's possible that they may have caused noises in the building that could have been misinterpreted as significant bangs or even footsteps. In addition, it is possible that the drop in temperature overnight could cause decaying wooden beams to contract and therefore make unexpected noises. What makes the place memorable, however, is its look and feel, especially at night. In fact we could both easily say that it is one of the scariest places we have ever been to and believe us, we've been to a lot of scary places in our time.

Conclusion

As we said earlier, if ever a place was likely to be haunted Château du Pays Lauragais would have to be a prime candidate, not just for its appearance and isolated location, but also for its chequered history. So often haunting phenomena are reported in locations with a troubled, tragic, violent or traumatic past. Remember the discussion on 'residual haunting', where events from the past impress themselves in the form of energy onto the very materials that make up the building? It's entirely possible that on the night of our investigation our apprehension may have refuelled the malevolent energy lurking in the château. If so, as well as giving us a spooky night to remember, it may have ensured that paranormal phenomena will continue to be reported there for many years to come.

Postscript

After our investigation of this mysterious derelict château, Ciarán discovered another intriguing slice of history associated with the place. During the Second World War there were various resistance movements active in the south-west of France. As well as fighting against the Germans, they built tunnels for escaped prisoners of war and crashed pilots to take them across the Pyrenees into the safety of Spain. Some of the tunnels lay south of Toulouse and there were persistent rumours that one tunnel originated at the Château du Pays Lauragais. We might have been standing above a Second World War escape tunnel. Could that explain the footsteps Yvette heard?

2

CHÂTEAU DE PUILAURENS

Haunting experiences can be reported almost anywhere – graveyards, houses, libraries, offices, shops – and a building does not have to be centuries old to be haunted. No book on ghost-hunting, however, feels complete without at least one mention of an old haunted castle. We had heard about just such a place while in the ancient fortified city of Carcassone; a mysterious lady in white was said to be haunting a castle in the area. Château De Puilaurens was just over an hour's drive directly south of where we were. We couldn't resist checking it out.

THE CASE OF THE CHÂTEAU DE PUILAURENS

Although it began life quite peacefully in the tenth century, when it was owned by the Abbey of Saint-Michel de Cuxa and the monks of the order lived there, Château de Puilaurens has a later history of conflict. This probably has quite a lot to do with its geographical location. It sits on high ground – 697 metres above sea level – with breathtaking views from its battlements of the mountains beyond. The Boulzane and Sainte Croix Valleys curve their way through these magnificent peaks, whose sides are covered with lush green conifers. The Spanish border is about 200 miles to the south, and about the same distance to the east lies the Mediterranean coast. It is hardly surprising that a castle commanding such a location has been used as a strategic military stronghold in several regional wars, including the Franco-Spanish War in the seventeenth century. Its most warlike period, though, was during the time of the Cathars.

The Cathars

The religious order of Catharism is thought to have its roots in Eastern Europe and the Byzantine empire, but it appeared in the Languedoc region of south-west France in the eleventh century. Its popularity grew during the twelfth century as it attracted more and more people, from all walks of life. Devotees rejected the material world and many of the trappings and dogma of the dominant Roman Catholic faith. One of the ways this manifested itself was in their refusal to contribute financially to the Catholic purse. Perhaps unsurprisingly then, at the beginning of the thirteenth century when the popularity of Catharism was at it height, the Catholic Church named its followers as heretics and the Pope led a Holy Army against them in a bid to wipe out this movement, which they considered heresy. Almost 600,000 men, women and children were slaughtered in this war.

Even though Catharism was, to all intents and purposes, completely wiped out as long ago as the end of the fourteenth century, our trip to the Languedoc region showed us that its influence is still visible in many ways. There are ruined Cathar castles of course, and historical records revealing the horrific details of the Cathar inquisition. Another hint that Catharism is in some way still alive is that, as you head south-east on the motorway, a sign on the approach to Carcassonne informs you that 'You are now entering Cathar Country'. There are even contemporary residents who identify themselves as Cathar. Interest in the Cathars' history and culture, and the region of France where it flourished, is currently at a high point due in no small part to bestselling books such as Kate Mosse's *Labyrinth* and Dan Brown's *The Da Vinci Code*.

Château de Puilaurens has had its fair share of gruesome tragedy and bloodshed. Perhaps the most well-known legend is the one that tells of an attempted massacre of thousands of Cathar priests, plus the women and children, from a town north of the castle. Many made their escape to Puilaurens and hid there. Following a siege, they were trapped inside its walls and then brutally massacred by soldiers following orders from their Catholic leaders. Not surprisingly, there have been numerous accounts over the years of strange feelings and ghostly occurrences, but the most notorious is the story of the lady in white.

Blanche de Bourbon

The apparition of a lady dressed in white has been reported. She is said to float around the castle and along the battlements. Unfortunately we couldn't locate any eyewitnesses, but it was clear from talking to some local residents that they were absolutely convinced that the castle was haunted and that it had been haunted for hundreds of years. Some locals thought the ghost was of a Cathar individual massacred at the castle all those centuries ago, while others believed that it was more likely to be the spectre of a high-born lady, Blanche de Bourbon, murdered there.

White Ladies

Sightings of White Ladies are frequently reported in old castles and stately homes. These apparitions are typically described as being beautiful and dressed in white from head to toe. They are similar to the phenomenon of 'Grey Ladies' that we discussed earlier in that it is often thought that these apparitions are of women who were murdered or died under other tragic circumstances, often as a result of the actions of a loved one. We have discovered, however, from our reading of historical cases and our own research, that White and Grey Ladies differ from each other in one very noticeable way: their social class. The majority of White Ladies appear in upper-class dwellings such as castles, manor houses and stately homes. It also appears from the records and our experience that most White Lady ghosts are identified with historical royals or noblewomen. There is the odd occasion when a lady from a noble background appears as a ghost of a different colour. For example, Lady Louisa Carteret is said to appear at Longleat House as a 'Green Lady'. Additionally, there is an interesting variation on the theme; there are suggestions that a 'lady haunting' begins with eyewitnesses seeing 'Blue' or 'Green' ladies but that over time the spectre's colour changes, turning white, then grey, before fading for ever. The bulk of the evidence, though, points to the difference between Grey and White Ladies being their social status.

Examples of White Lady haunting figures, all of whom have a royal or upper-class background, are Lady Campbell at Glamis Castle; Lady Blanche de Warenne at Rochester Castle; Lady Christian Nimmo, who was mistress to Corstorphine Castle's Laird, James Forrester; the 'White Lady of Berlin', who is reputedly the ghost of Countess Agnes of Orlamunde, and, perhaps the most famous of all: Queen Catherine Howard, wife of the infamous Henry VIII, at Hampton Court Palace.

Blanche de Bourbon certainly fits the classic 'White Lady' profile of a noblewoman meeting a tragic end. Although Blanche did not actually die at Puilaurens, it appears that her stay at Puilaurens as an unmarried woman may have been the last happy event of her life. Legend has it that within days of her marriage to Pedro of Castile, or Peter the Cruel as he was frequently and ominously known, he had tired of her. He ordered her imprisonment, and she was incarcerated for eight years before being assassinated on her husband's orders. Reports differ as to how she was killed; some say that she was shot with a crossbow and arrow, while others claim that she was poisoned. Either way, her tragic end has left a ghostly legacy at Puilaurens, a legacy that is impossible to avoid since the castle's western tower was named La Tour de la Dame Blanche (White Lady Tower) after her.

We both knew that the phenomena reported at Château de Puilaurens could potentially be explained away by the possible influence on the public's imagination of the irresistible combination of ghostly tales of White Ladies and the ruined castle with its tragic past. But there was only one way to find out for sure if the château was haunted, and that was to visit it and carry out an investigation ourselves.

Our Investigation Begins

As we drive south along a deserted windy road, we spy Château de Puilaurens perched imposingly on its hilltop. The full impact of how high up it is, though, doesn't hit us until we park the car and look up at its looming bulk. We pay the entrance fee and begin our steep climb.

Ciarán: *This is stunning. The photographs of the castle really don't do it justice. It is surrounded by the most beautiful countryside. Roads meander their way through valleys with precarious rocks overhanging every turn. It was a bit frightening getting here as the roads are very narrow and at one point we had to do a three-point turn when we realised we'd taken a wrong turning. This is going to be some climb getting up to the castle. We're approaching it from the west side, hiking along very steep paths carved through the dense undergrowth with botanical highlights indicated at various points.*

Yvette: *Phew! After a day exploring Carcassonne and the surrounding area I didn't expect to end it mountain-climbing! Just kidding – this is an amazing place. On the way here I think we came across only one other car, there's just nobody around. I can't wait to see the view from up there. Right, it's time to get the heart pumping and the legs moving. As we get closer to the stone walls of the castle you can really appreciate how steep and high it is. My thighs can certainly attest to the difficulty of the climb! The closer we get the less vegetation there is and the more the path weaves its way round huge boulders. At one point we have to literally climb over ruined walls before we reach what would have been an entrance gate.*

Slightly out of breath after our climb, the three of us (Ciarán's wife Gaëlle is here to help us with recording) take a few moments to look around, and observe that the castle, although clearly beaten and battered, is still fairly well preserved and rather impressive. We both agree that it feels as if time has stood still here. Our modern gear – backpacks, cameras and contemporary clothing – feel strangely out of place in this setting; we feel as though we should be wearing monks' habits or knights' armour, either praying for forgiveness or defending the ramparts! We're also delighted to see that the place is deserted, which will make our investigation much easier. The courtyard is before us, stretching almost the entire length of the building. Looking at our plan of the castle, we see that it measures approximately seventy by twenty-five metres. It's vast.

Tingling with that familiar sense of anticipation that we always get at the beginning of a ghost hunt, we agree that the best way to start will be to stand here in the courtyard, the main central space of the castle, and soak up the atmosphere. Yvette suggests reading out an ancient invocation, the idea being that it might attract spirit energy. Yvette chooses one that she thinks may have been familiar to the Cathars.

We have to say here that we are not going to reveal the chant in this book as we feel it would not be appropriate to do so. Yvette believes that invocations should only be used by those with considerable experience.

Invocations

Invocations have long been condemned, by cynics and believers alike, because of the belief that they may create a link to dark forces. If you look up the word 'invocation' in the dictionary, one definition may be that they 'summon up the devil', although there will almost certainly be other, more innocuous definitions.

Individuals with a strong belief in spirit communication may be hypersensitive to the possibility of negative influences finding a way through, and interpret the slightest negative event as the result of an invocation. At the other end of the belief spectrum, a sceptic could still be vulnerable in a psychological way, possibly finding their unconscious fears coming to the surface. Ciarán, with his approach and beliefs that are so different to Yvette's, does feel that the simple act of verbally invoking spirits can make those involved highly suggestible and exposed and, therefore, open to such psychological pressures. Interestingly enough, it is very rare to come across accounts in the media of positive experiences with invocations. Anecdotally, too, there seem to be more reports of negative experiences than of positive ones.

David Wells, the medium who has advised Yvette on this topic, repeatedly advocates the seriousness of using invocations; they are not to be used lightly. If, however, you are determined to try out invocations, Yvette has learned the following guidelines:

> Begin your invocation by announcing that the session will only allow positive experiences and that negative energies are not welcome.

> Do not ask for physical signs. Simply ask the spirits to make their presence felt to you in a harmless way.

> When you are done, end the invocation. THIS IS A VERY IMPORTANT STEP.

> When you are finished say goodbye and thank you and announce that you are closing the session.

Ciarán: *Following Yvette's instructions, we have just read out an invocation in Latin. According to some mediums this can encourage spirits to manifest themselves. The use of invocations is an ancient tradition that has reference points in many cultures. I love the history of this sort of thing, tracing it back through ancient cultures such as the Egyptians or Mayans, but I feel a bit uncomfortable actually doing it. Another, similar technique is to produce a note using a singing bowl. This is supposedly to do with tapping into a particular natural frequency, perhaps the Earth's resonant frequency. It sounds suspiciously like pseudoscience to me! Another frequency-related approach that I've heard of is to produce a high-pitched scream. Perhaps I should ask Yvette to do one of her bloodcurdling squeals; but then again that might frighten the spirits away!*

Yvette: *I feel a bit odd chanting in an open space like this and I think Ciarán does too. I do believe in the power of words and sounds to attract energy, so let's see what happens. Having said that, I think we could be wasting our time as it is very rare to get activity in a huge open space like this. The occasional echo that our voices are producing is a bit disconcerting. We need to find somewhere more enclosed, more protected from the wind. The wind is quite strong up here and this makes it hard to pick up any auditory phenomena. I'm going to suggest to Ciarán that we move towards the South Tower.*

As we head over to the South Tower we notice a postern on the south-east wall. Posterns were originally created for use as small alternative entrances in castles, often just big enough to let one person pass through at a time. They were frequently hidden so that they could be used during sieges or times of war. We speculate that this is exactly the reason for the existence of this postern, because had we not been looking carefully we would probably never have noticed it.

Yvette: *This is much better than standing in the courtyard. We can actually listen out for noises now. No, it can't be that quick! I just heard a noise to my left, like a thump, and I have no idea what that could be. I could also have sworn that while we were walking towards the tower Gaëlle was beside me as I chanted, but when I turned to look she was filming us from further back in the courtyard. Perhaps there is something to this chanting business after all!*

Ciarán: *We've now entered the South Tower and I'm starting to get more excited. Yvette just told me that she thought someone was walking beside her as we walked towards the tower. Also, from the tower's entrance you can really see the extent of the castle and how much ground we have to cover. You can just imagine archers standing at these windows, not giving invaders any opportunity to advance. The atmosphere is different here compared to the courtyard. It's slightly cooler to start with, but that may be because there's little chance of sunlight entering. It's certainly quieter, and I know that there's no wind in here, but it feels eerily calm.*

We start hunting for other enclosed areas, occasionally chanting the invocation together as we go, hoping that it will attract spirits. We pause for a while and Yvette starts calling out. We admire the impressive acoustics of the place. Yvette thinks for a moment that she hears a loud sigh, but we both agree that it is probably the wind howling in the massive courtyard. The wind is pretty strong up here. We wait in silence for a few minutes to confirm our theory. After a couple of minutes we hear the same sound again and nod knowingly to each other.

After exploring for a while we find exactly the enclosed space we've been looking for. It's next to another postern on the north wall and is a cave-like structure. The entrance is a simple hole and we have to help each other in order to climb into it. You wouldn't have any chance of a quick escape from here! Inside, it's surprisingly dry and warm and we wonder what this room might once have been. The roof is arched and the far end appears to be bricked up with more modern-looking bricks than the other walls. We both call out for any spirits to show themselves, then listen, but apart from the muffled sound of the howling wind outside we can't hear anything. We decide that as we are out of the wind and everything is so quiet here it might be an ideal place to cast some runes.

Casting the Runes

On our way here we had already decided to do a rune casting because we felt that the archaic origins of this ritual suited the age of the château. There are fewer instances of runic writing in the countries of continental Europe than in the Nordic countries, the area most strongly associated with runes, but the history of runic writing extends back many centuries and a variation of the runic alphabet would have been used very widely in Europe in the medieval period. It is perhaps a long shot to suppose that any spirits associated with this castle would understand a medieval runic alphabet, not to mention want to communicate through it, but it is probably more likely than them understanding the way we speak.

Rune-casting

Casting the runes is a very ancient method of divination. Although there is historical proof of a runic alphabet originating around 2000 years ago, the history and origin of the use of runes for guidance, prediction and healing are less clear. Certainly the earliest use of runes as a divination method is open to speculation, although there are some references to this belief as far back as the sixth and seventh centuries.

The runic alphabet is thought to have originated with the ancient Norsemen, partly because the symbols are letters from an ancient Nordic alphabet and runes are frequently mentioned in old Nordic literature. According to legend, the runes came about as a result of a bizarre ceremony conducted by the Norse god Odin, the god of wisdom and war. He impaled himself on Yggdrasil, the 'World Tree' at the centre of the universe in the ancient Norse belief system, and hung there for nine days and nights. It was this extreme form of shamanistic sacrifice that gave him his unsurpassed mystical knowledge of the runes.

Before we talk about our rune-casting at the château, let's first explore some theories about how it works. One theory is that the unconscious mind somehow influences the positioning of the runes. According to this theory, the unconscious watches the progress of the diviner (the person casting the runes) very carefully, and actually controls the motions of the diviner's hands so that the runes fall in a particular way. Whether this is in fact possible has not yet been subjected to rigorous experimentation.

Another idea is to do with the action of spirits. The theory here is that the spirits are the influencing force; the diviner may actively communicate with them and ask for their guidance in revealing a runic message, or they may exert influence without the diviner being aware of their presence.

A rational explanation for rune-casting is that it's similar to 'retro-fitting' or finding a concrete structure in what is actually complete randomness. Think of the Rorschach inkblot tests used in psychology. They are completely random and yet different people find different shapes and meanings in them. In the same way, this theory goes, if you are actively looking for some sort of structure or message in the runes, you will find it. Ciarán favours this explanation and is very fond of Robert T. Carroll's writings on the subject, which are extracted below.

How is it that random alphabetic stone selection can be so useful? Easy! Anything can be a source of trans-formation and breakthrough if you decide to let it be. Runes, tarot cards, the I Ching, enneagrams, Myers-Briggs . . . anything can be used to stimulate self-reflection and self-analysis. Anything can be used to justify coming to a decision about an unresolved matter. Coming to a deci-sion brings relief, reduces anxiety, and may well seem like a breakthrough and transformation. In other words, using a method like rune stones or tarot to help you make your decision relieves you of the responsibility for it. The choice was made for you by the stones and your subconscious mind, so you are off the hook if anything goes wrong. Furthermore, since there is no standard interpretation of any of this stuff, you can always change your initial inter-pretation to fit new facts or desires. When you are the oracle yourself, it is always a win-win situation.

Where do we stand with all this? As always, somewhere in the middle! Yvette leans towards the supernatural explanation and Ciarán towards the rational expla-nation, but both of us accept the possibility that the unconscious may play a significant part. In other words, we believe that to work with the runes you need to use your intuition, whatever you think that actually is, and work out what the symbols mean to you. There are numerous books on the subject, the majority of them 'how-to' guides. Do be aware that they differ quite widely in their interpretations.

Back to our rune-casting at Château de Puilaurens. Ciarán casts the stones three times. On the first two throws the symbol Kenaz lands outside the main grouping. On the third throw the symbol Ansuz lands away from the group. Because of their isolation from the rest of the runes, we focus our attention on these two symbols.

Ansuz represents communication – something we were trying to do – and also the wind. As we'd already discovered in the courtyard, this place is most certainly a wind trap! Kenaz is the symbol for fire, and fire can transform and enlighten but also destroy and kill. We can't think of a stone that more accurately sums up the persecution of the Cathars at Château de Puilaurens.

It's easy to argue that we were both seeing what we wanted to see as we interpreted the runes and that we could have convinced ourselves of the significance of whichever rune had landed away from the main group. Of course this is possible, but then again there are plenty of other runes, or groupings of runes, that would not have seemed as appropriate as the ones that our reading produced.

Yvette: *The enclosure we are standing in is really creepy; there's some writing on the wall and I haven't a clue what it says. I don't know why but I feel as it there is something underneath us. It feels as though the floor beneath my feet could give way at any moment and reveal another room or enclosure, or perhaps a grave! I'd love to know what was once under here. I'm not scared but I feel odd, like there is something constantly looking at my back. I know in parapsychology they call this the 'Staring Effect'. It's that feeling when you think somebody is looking at the back of your head and you turn around and they actually are, only in this case there's nobody behind me.*

The rune-casting was great but I'm not drawing any conclusions yet. There were so many runic symbols on the ground that it was difficult to examine every single one. If we had someone who specialised in reading runes they may be able to tell us immediately what was being said. At least Ciarán is taking a photograph of each casting and there is also a film recording of it. As I said I'm not scared; it's like I've got butterflies and am waiting for something to happen. Now this is quite something! Gaëlle has been filming us doing the rune-casting from outside the enclosure and her camera has just switched itself off for no reason. It hasn't done that before and there are hours of battery life left in it. It would be a good idea now to ask the spirits here to do it again, to influence the camera.

Ciarán: *As a parapsychologist the most important thing for me is always to keep an open, questioning mind and that's why I think it's okay to experiment with mystical techniques such as invocation and divination, and in this case rune-casting. Call it coincidence, but it was great that we got the rune most associated with death and destruction and the rune associated with communication between this world and the next in our casts. I simply scattered the runes out of the bag and these two just distanced themselves from the group. I'm impressed – not convinced, but impressed. My scepticism with the runes comes from my college years in the States giving readings to friends. I realised that it didn't matter what the runes said or what I said. As long as I was giving information to the person that was vague and ambiguous, they filled in the gaps.*

Although I try to remain sceptical, and always question until I see convincing evidence, when someone close to me has an unusual experience it is more difficult to explain away. Gaëlle was patiently filming our rune-casting, responding to our movements and pointing the camera to ensure we had a record of every occurrence. She suddenly reported that the camera 'died'. It had apparently switched off of its own accord. My natural reaction would be to question the account and double-check that it had actually been recording, or question whether it had accidentally been switched off. When it is your wife reporting the experience though, it is more difficult to question. Despite this, I would question even my own judgement when it comes to reporting something paranormal, and now even Gaëlle is unsure of whether she accidentally hit the on/off switch. Or is that just me influencing her?

White Lady Tower

The light is starting to fade and we are both surprised that the time has passed so quickly. It feels as if we've only been here a short while, but in fact two hours have already flown by, as if time had simply vanished. As we climb out of the enclosure and walk under the archway towards the keep, we glance across the courtyard. It has now taken on a very different feel. It is eerily quiet and with the fading light, definitely spooky. Shooting fleeting glances towards the South Tower, now about thirty metres away, our nervousness increases as shadows start to form. The castle walls start to close in a bit. It's just an optical illusion, caused at least in part by the rising moon, but it makes us move a little faster. We don't want to be here all night; if anything were to happen, getting help would be very difficult. We decide to make our way to the White Lady Tower, or Tour de la Dame Blanche. Maybe Blanche will show herself there.

Yvette: *We're in the White Lady Tower and it's far too quiet in here for me. I really want something to happen, the White Lady to show herself, even a noise to respond* to my calling out. I feel a bit depressed and I'm not sure why. Maybe I should say dispirited! It's not because nothing is happening, I was fine before I got here, but now I feel like crying. If it was pitch-black outside and we were here later at night I know I would be terrified. I'll try throwing some stones to see if the spirits throw something back. If that doesn't work I know that there's a loudhailer that runs from the ground floor of the tower up to the second floor. Kind of like an ancient speaker or walkie-talkie system. Essentially it is a tube that was hollowed out of the brick wall as the tower was constructed. If someone stands on the ground floor and speaks into one end of the tube, another person standing on the second floor can hear the words as if they are said by someone standing right next to them.

Ciarán: Yvette is throwing stones and, interestingly, it looks as if something is coming back on my camera; it could of course be dust particles. We did kick up some dust just by walking in here. I also feel a slight headache coming on. Now Yvette is jumping out of her skin because she heard a loud bang. I'm sorry, there's really nothing to worry about because it's just the back of my torch falling off! This hasn't happened before though and I've had this torch for almost a year. It's peculiar that it should come off like that because you need to screw it on several times and I know I screwed it on tight when I last changed the batteries. How weird. I can't explain that but maybe I'm reaching for something unusual to happen. Not *tightening it all these months may be the clue. Either way it has certainly got Yvette scared! Psychics and mediums believe that ghosts can move objects or influence electrical equipment. Other people think that highly sensitive people can subconsciously influence material objects. It's akin to a process called psychokinesis or telekinesis (if you've seen the film* Carrie *you'll know what I'm talking about) and is a field of great interest to me, whether it is caused by ghosts or not.*

Gaëlle stays with Yvette as she whispers into a groove in the wall, the point where the loudhailer begins. She's whispering requests to the spirits, as if she's trying to coax them out of their hiding places. Ciarán moves to a different area and starts a lone vigil, but he doesn't remain on his own for long because Yvette and Gaëlle, who are a little spooked, return. They had heard a brief whisper in response to Yvette's. The whisper was indecipherable but they were adamant that it had definitely happened; both of them were sure that they heard it. We head back to the tower to see if it happens again, but to no avail. Ciarán thinks he may have heard a distant whisper but then puts it down to an echo – or even the loudhailer just doing what it's meant to!

Ciarán: *Yvette has suggested we split up and so I head to the keep. It's quite large and rises up between the north-west tower and the Tour de la Dame Blanche where Yvette and Gaëlle have stayed. Being on my own*

*in here doesn't faze me at all. The headache I had earlier
has gone now. Could've been slight dehydration and
taking that swig from a water bottle on the walk over
to the keep cured it. Oh! What was that? Just Yvette
coming in, nothing ghostly! She heard a whisper back
in the tower and is a little spooked but actually more
intrigued than really scared. I think as the lights go down
we're becoming more susceptible to our own imagination.
Perhaps our minds are starting to play tricks on us.*

Yvette: *In the tower I was asking for the White Lady to
show herself or communicate in some way. I asked for
her to whisper her name to me. Suddenly I heard a very
slight whisper. I couldn't hear what was said but it is
enough for me to go and get Ciarán and hope that he
would experience the same thing. That's the frustrating
thing about working with Ciarán. My experience now
becomes an anecdote unless he experiences the same
thing. Well, I know I heard something!*

Conclusion

After taking a walk along the western battlements,
admiring the awe-inspiring view, we head back down
into the courtyard, which is now illuminated only by
moonlight. Out here the sky is very clear and there
is no light pollution. The stars stare brightly down at
us and this almost eases our nerves as we collect our
thoughts and decide to leave the castle.

We both feel a little unnerved as we leave the tower

and start to make our way down the hill back to the car. Although we didn't see the White Lady, the investigation has certainly given us a lot to think about. Yvette thinks that the staring energy she felt when we were casting the runes, and her low mood in the White Lady Tower, were both significant. Ciarán is intrigued by the torch incident and also by the rune-casting; but intrigued in his usual sceptical way! It's been an experiment for us to use invocations and runes in our investigations and we will certainly think about using them again.

We wouldn't say we found the château scary as such, but we did find the atmosphere odd and intense. There was an almost religious feel to the place and you could practically picture in your mind individuals from long ago, deep in their meditation and prayer. We were very aware of the layers of history we were stepping into; that awareness could have explained Yvette's sense of presence in the enclosed area and the change of mood in the White Lady Tower. As for the camera switching off for no reason and the end of Ciarán's torch falling off, there are possible logical explanations, such as faults in the equipment or Ciarán not screwing on the torch lid properly. It's all a little too coincidental for Yvette, though.

The eeriness of the howling wind and the way it whispered through the castle walls, plus the way our voices echoed several times in the open spaces, have made an impression on us. But could these whispers and echoes have been voices from the past? After spending several hours drinking in the atmosphere of the place, imagining its centuries-old residents going about their business, we're sure you will understand why we left Château de Puilaurens feeling as if they were.

3

THE MYSTERY OF RENNES LE CHÂTEAU

Fresh from visiting Château de Puilaurens, one of the last Cathar strongholds, and with just a few days left in France to carry out our investigations, we were both keen to continue exploring this region of France with its Cathar heritage. Like millions of others, we had both read Dan Brown's *The Da Vinci Code* and been hooked by the fascinating and intricate plot. But was it all based on fact, or was it just fantasy? We hoped that by doing an investigation of our own at Rennes le Château, the tiny village at the very heart of the mystery, we'd be able to better understand the story and come to our own conclusions. Although the book doesn't directly reference the village, there are numerous references to the story, enough to attract visitors to it. The main link is the priest at the centre of the controversy, Father Berenger Saunière. In *The Da Vinci Code*, the main character, Robert Langdon, is on the trail of the murderer of a curator called Jacques Saunière.

THE CASE OF RENNES LE CHÂTEAU

For those unfamiliar with the story, or in need of a brief recap, the legend dates from the late 1800s when Father Berenger Saunière was appointed to the small village of Rennes le Château in south-west France which at the time had about 300 inhabitants. His first job was the restoration of the sixth-century church in the centre of the village, a job he did admirably. During the building work things got very interesting. Supposedly, Saunière found some parchments hidden in a pillar underneath the altar. The information contained on the parchments was coded but the priest believed it to be of sufficient importance that he consulted his superiors, first in Carcassone, then in Paris. Although there is no record of what was discussed in these meetings, the visits resulted in a previously lowly priest returning to the tiny village a wealthy man. He spent large amounts of money building a tower called La Tour Magdala and increasing his library stock, not to mention adding expensive decoration to his church. The majority of the money, though, was spent on himself and an increasingly lavish lifestyle.

The story grew in fame in the latter half of the 1900s, with treasure-hunters and various adventure-seekers all trying to uncover the source of Saunière's wealth. The mayor of the village had to intervene at one point because there was so much tunnelling going on under the village foundations that houses were in danger of subsiding. There exist, to this day, remnants of those treasure-seekers' tunnels.

It was clear that these ancient parchments meant something – but what? Saunière had obviously discovered something in them that resulted in him becoming so wealthy. Perhaps his treasure was of such value to his superiors that they paid him a great deal of money for it. Or, possibly, what he knew was so inflammatory that his silence had to be bought.

We were really eager to find out as much as we could on this investigation, since there are so many fascinating myths and questions that have been built up around Rennes le Château over the years. We both love a good mystery and we couldn't think of a better way to finish our ghost-hunting trip to France than with an investigation of perhaps the greatest supernatural mystery ever told.

Ciarán: *I'm immediately sceptical about this particular story. Although I've read the book* The Da Vinci Code *and heard of its connections to the Saunière story, I was very clear while reading it that I was reading a work of fiction. It would be easy to get drawn in, perhaps, because of the claim that some of the story was true. I know of the other version of the story about Saunière's wealth, but I'm determined to keep it quiet and not discuss it with Yvette until after our visit because I don't want to cloud her judgement.*

The journey up to the village is a very long one. The road is incredibly winding and some of the locals coming down are going at such a speed I think they have a death wish!

Yvette: *I'm excited about visiting the village as it feels like a once-in-a-lifetime opportunity. The drive here is the main reason why I won't be popping back in the near future. It's gorgeous scenery but there is nothing around and we are miles and miles from anywhere. I think it's over two hours from Toulouse. The story about Saunière's mysterious wealth has intrigued me ever since heard about it around the time when I was reading* The Da Vinci Code. *It was more what the actual parchments said that I thought was the key and the connection to the novel. In the novel it's all about Mary Magdalene being Jesus's wife and I wondered if that's exactly what was on the parchments.*

Our Investigation Begins

It's very early in the morning and we are driving slowly up the mountain towards Rennes le Château. We find it hard to take in the breathtaking views and country-side on our way up as the road is so narrow it seems that we could career off it at any moment with the slightest swerve of the steering wheel.

When we arrive we are the only people in sight, which doesn't surprise us as we know that the village only has a population of 125. The first hint of civilisation is a white dog lounging in the sun, but a few minutes later another group of visitors arrive behind us, and then another, and another.

We find the museum where Saunière's church of Mary Magdalene is located, and take a good look around. Ciarán is particularly interested in an exhibit of the pillar where the parchments were discovered. We then head towards the church, where we are first in line, until the doors open. As we enter the place we're hit by how creepy it is, a feeling not helped by the eerie statue of the Devil inside the door that seems to stare piercingly at you as soon as you enter! The words carved by the door are pretty off-putting too: 'Terribilis est locus iste' ('This place is terrifying').

The church is everything we had hoped; lavish, enigmatic and colourful, and with odd features that seem designed for the purpose of puzzling the visitor. The inclusion of the Devil by the door, for example, is an odd decision. In addition, statues of people who we initially assume are Joseph and Mary, each holding a baby Jesus in their arms, stand on either side of the altar. Could these in fact be statues of Jesus and Mary Magdalene? But the thing we both find the most intriguing is the sacristy and another section of the building that both appear, at first glance, to be hidden once you enter the church. It reminds us of investigations we've done in the past, of castles where you can stand outside and count the number of exterior windows but then go inside, recount, and find one or two missing. It means that somewhere there is a hidden room!

These two sections of the church, though, turn out not to be as exciting as we originally thought. Although they are slightly hidden within the church, the sacristy can be accessed via a door. The 'hidden' section turns out to be quite mundane and is a small room that appears to serve no purpose. It appears too small to store anything and is quite dilapidated and bare of decoration. The sacristy holds a beautiful stained-glass window that momentarily transfixes us. Yvette is particularly mesmerised by its representation of Mary Magdalene.

Yvette: *The more I walk around this village and look at the church, the more I feel that the information contained on the parchments did have something to do with Mary Magdalene. The very fact that the tower built by Saunière is called the Tower of Magdalene, and the fact that we have found out that the church was originally dedicated to her back in 1059, both seem to be clues to the contents of those parchments. Then when you look at the décor in the church, the statues, the stained-glass window . . . it's all confirming my hypothesis. There you go Ciarán, starting to sound bookish!*

Ciarán: *This is a lovely little village but I'm not seeing anything that makes me think there's a great religious mystery hidden here. I can remember reading as a teenager the book that originally put forward the idea that Mary Magdalene and Jesus married, had a family and moved to southern France. According to the authors, the secret was guarded by a religious sect called the Priory of Sion, another detail that Dan Brown's book also picks up on. The connection between this mystery and Saunière in the book I read is that the documents he discovered stated this fact and told the reader where to find the bodies of the family. Some have even said that Saunière actually discovered the burial ground of Jesus. What we have found today, speaking to the local bookshop owner, is that it is definitely a fact that Saunière accumulated great wealth. I think, however, it might be time to tell Yvette the alternative story, the one that I think is more plausible.*

Though the story of Saunière, the Priory of Sion and the controversy surrounding Mary Magdalene have enthralled many people over recent decades, the truth is possibly a little more mundane. It is said that in the 1950s the owner of the Villa Bethania, who had turned it into a restaurant, deliberately circulated the story of Saunière's wealth in the hope of attracting the business of customers looking for a good mystery. His motivation makes perfect sense if you look at the geographical location of the village. Nobody would pass through here on their way to Spain or Andorra. There are other, easier, routes to take if you want to travel further south. In 1956 the tale supposedly attracted the attention of a gentleman by the name of Pierre Plantard, who was responsible for the creation of the Priory of Sion through forging documents. The Priory of Sion is often described and thought of as an ancient institution, traceable back thousands of years, but according to this story it was nothing more mysterious than a 1950s hoax! Plantard is said to have then enlisted the help of an author to write a book claiming that Saunière had found religious treasure.

Hearing both sides of the story seemed to just add to the enigmas and puzzles surrounding this place. We'd have loved to do an all-night vigil in the church or cemetery, preferably with a medium, but obtaining permission would have been hard if not impossible. All we could do was take a look, drink in the atmosphere and, like every other curious visitor here, draw our own conclusions about the place.

Conclusion

Ciarán: *Before visiting Rennes le Château, the cult of Mary Magdalene as depicted by Dan Brown had drawn me in, but at the same time I was keenly aware that this was a legendary, possibly fictional version of the story. However, it soon became clear to me that the facts are quite different.*

Let's begin with the so-called hollow pillar that contained those crucial documents. While visiting the museum I noticed that if you look closely, you can see that the pillar is not hollow at all. In fact it has only a very small hole. I'm not convinced that any parchments could have been squeezed into there.

There is documentation to show that Saunière made a note in his diary of a discovery he made while doing the renovation. He tried to keep it secret in order to make himself some money from selling the objects he found, which were possibly Visigothic artefacts. He also probably started to excavate the church's surroundings, hoping to find more. But on examining the evidence I really don't think that this was the only source of Saunière's wealth. Doing research of my own while visiting the area, I found out that a Catholic investigation at the time revealed Saunière to be charging for his services. This entailed practices such as receiving money to conduct a service for a named soul, which was believed to ensure that their soul ascended to heaven. Saunière supposedly conducted thousands of these services. They would indeed have brought him great wealth, but as a result he was eventually suspended from his post.

I believe that Saunière probably made his money from selling masses illegally rather than being paid off or otherwise profiting from the discovery of inflammatory materials. This conclusion leaves another question though: why on earth invent such a story about Christ and Mary Magdalene? Perhaps simply the controversy of it would be enough to provoke interest. The idea has now appeared in so many books, articles and documentaries that I feel sure it is a legend that'll never die.

So, I remain highly sceptical of Saunière having found any great treasure. The other version of the story seems so much more plausible. The problem is that as each year passes the number of visitors increases and the legends become part of a sort of universal game of Chinese whispers where the truth gets shrouded by many fictional versions. Although there is of course the saying that truth is much stranger than the fiction. I think so anyway!

Yvette: *Days after my trip to Rennes le Château I still couldn't stop thinking about the sacristy and that stained-glass window. As soon as I stepped inside I was held spellbound by the atmosphere of mystery, intrigue and suspense that hangs in the air. You could say I'm being influenced by all the media interest created by* The Da Vinci Code, *but I really tried to remain objective and the church itself didn't blow me away as I thought it might. It was intriguing all right but I didn't get a sense of wonder. I only got tingles down my spine when I stepped inside the sacristy and saw that magnificent stained-glass window. It just hypnotised me and I could have stared at it for hours. For a split second everything around me vanished; it was as if the world melted away. I've never had an experience like that before or since. I could go on and on with questions and thoughts about the stained-glass window. Every time I think about it my mind races with more ideas*

Ciarán remains sceptical, but after leaving Rennes le Château I believe that the answer to the world's greatest mystery could very well be in that window. Ask me why I think this and I'd find it hard to say, but it's got something to do with the feeling of awe, anticipation and total absorption that I got when I stared at the barely lit image in the sacristy. I'm well aware that feelings do not constitute proof and won't ever hold up to scientific scrutiny, but in a case like this, when there are so many convincing arguments for and against, feelings or gut instinct may be the only way for me to sum up.

Both of us came to Rennes le Château with an open mind about the Jesus and Mary Magdalene theory, and we both left with the same attitude, although I was more inclined to believe that Christ once lived and died here with Mary Magdalene and Ciarán was more inclined to disbelieve. Not much help for you, the reader, looking for answers, I know, but I hope it will encourage you to do your own research, expand your horizons, perhaps even visit the church for yourself and, like all good paranormal investigators, keep your mind open to the amazing possibilities.

4

THE WINCHESTER
MYSTERY HOUSE

There was a pause, an expectant silence in the room. With the volume this high, the first few seconds of the recording were just a noisy hiss, the usual kind of static that you'd expect from a cheap digital recorder. Despite this, here, maybe, was the proof we had been searching for.

'Is there anybody here? Please can you talk to me?' Yvette's pleading voice rang in the air.

Silence for about five seconds. Neither of us could breathe.

'Please talk to me, let me know that you're here, tell me your name.'

A brief pause, then in hushed tones came the answer. 'Elizabeth.'

MYSTERIOUS BY NAME . . .[?]

When a location has the word 'mystery' included in its name, you've got to be sceptical. But this is California, the home of theme parks, big cars, malls and Hollywood. In this part of the country, people don't tend to do things by halves. When they have something to be proud of, an interesting story to tell, a history to sell, they shout about it. So here was the Winchester Mystery House, a labyrinthine 160-room building that has not so much grown as exploded outwards from its original eight rooms, the result of a bizarre crusade by its seemingly eccentric owner, Sarah Lockwood Winchester.

Yvette: *Okay let's be honest. This place is weird. We haven't gone inside yet but just seeing it for the first time and seeing where it is in the town is bizarre. We're staying in the centre of San José, on a gorgeous main street stuffed with trendy restaurants, cafés and bars. The street and pavements are permanently clean, the cars make you drool, and everyone looks like they're auditioning for a part in* Melrose Place. *On our walk here Ciarán got so excited – he said he saw Giovanni Ribisi, an actor he swears I'd have recognised if I'd seen him. The end of the street widened out and across the road was a huge car park and mall. At first we thought we were lost, but then we spied the Winchester Mystery*

House. It rises out of its lush green garden like a turn-of-the-century European greeting card. The haphazard roofs are in stark contrast to the flat-topped malls and office buildings that surround it. In any environment it would be striking, but here it is spectacular!

Ciarán: I had seen photos of the Winchester Mystery House before arriving in the US. I had even seen a televised investigation of the place by an American team of ghost hunters. Despite this, nothing could prepare me for seeing it in the flesh. It really is spectacular, though odd at the same time. You can really see the influence from Europe. The only time I've seen something similar was on a trip to the Yucatán area of Mexico. In the capital, Mérida, there is a long street stretching north, the Paseo de Montejo, where grand mansions owned by the rich landowners of the time were built in a late-nineteenth-century European style. Each person built their mansion more magnificent and pompous than the last in an attempt to outdo their neighbour. The Winchester Mystery House would have fitted in perfectly. A truly stunning sight, but what secrets and delights would the inside hold?

The 'Eccentric' Mrs Winchester

Sarah Lockwood Winchester has been variously described as 'eccentric', 'inscrutable' 'intelligent', 'a Spiritualist', 'innovative', 'a recluse' and 'mad'. Having researched the history behind Sarah Winchester and her fabulous house, we believe the most appropriate adjective would be 'fascinating'.

Sarah Winchester was married to William Wirt Winchester and they lived in New Haven, Connecticut. William was heir to the fortune of the famous Winchester rifle company. His death in 1881, following his father's the year before, meant that Sarah was left with half of the company and a personal daily income of around USD$1000, a pretty dizzying amount even today, let alone in the nineteenth century. Although there are records of her family history, and numerous historical accounts of the gun company, Sarah's move to California in the mid-1880s and her development of the Winchester Mystery House is shrouded in uncertainty. One explanation for Sarah's purchase of the house, and its subsequent expansion, could be her grief following the death of several family members.

Her only child, Annie Pardee, died in 1866, at only a few weeks old, from the horrible disease marasmus. This severe form of malnutrition can reduce a child to less than eighty per cent of their healthy weight and yet curse the victim with a voracious appetite. Around fifteen years later Sarah lost her father-in-law, Oliver Winchester, then, just a year later in 1881, her husband died of tuberculosis. It would hardly be surprising if Sarah had slipped into depression after helplessly watching her only child die that horrific death. Her husband and father-in-law dying relatively soon afterwards would have only added to this still-potent grief.

As the story has it, after this series of shattering events Sarah was given advice by friends, or perhaps a local doctor – the records are not completely clear on the details. It's not hard to imagine that this advice could have been along the lines of, 'Get a change of scenery, go somewhere warm and find a hobby to keep you busy'. Whatever the explanation, Sarah moved west in 1884 and purchased the unfinished eight-room farmhouse near San José. Her 'hobby' was to build and build, increasing the number of floors, adding extensions, all, astonishingly, without the aid of an architect. For this reason the house features many structural and design oddities, such as doors that open onto walls, trapdoors, blocked chimneys, barred windows and stairs that lead nowhere. There are also forty-seven fireplaces, thirteen bathrooms and six kitchens. Sarah continued adding elements to the house until her death in 1922.

The supernatural story behind Sarah and the Winchester house has become more widely known than the more mundane version, and is by far the more engrossing one. It begins with Sarah, no doubt grieving for the loved ones she had recently lost, deciding that the deaths were some sort of family curse. She visited a Boston-based medium by the name of Adam Coons, who confirmed her ideas, telling her that the Winchester family was cursed and that the spirit of everyone ever killed by a Winchester rifle was seeking revenge. The only way Sarah could make amends, Coons told her, was by buying a house and constantly expanding it. One version of the story relates that Coons told her that the rooms she added would house the fallen spirits, before concluding with the ominous order, 'As long as you build, you will live. Stop and you will die!'

Another version of the story has Sarah deciding, or being persuaded, that she must construct a mansion with a maze of rooms in order to trap and confuse the spirits and keep them from harming her. Either way, this legend certainly comes to the forefront of your mind when you are first confronted with the interior and its veritable labyrinth of rooms, windows, doors and stairs.

THE CASE OF THE WINCHESTER MYSTERY HOUSE

The tales of the supernatural surrounding this house are said to have begun back in 1884, as soon as Sarah Winchester arrived. The locals immediately began to speculate (or gossip!) about her reason for being there, and their interest and the air of strangeness it created around the house was exacerbated by the fact that neighbours regularly heard the chiming of a bell coming from the house, always at midnight and 2 a.m. Do these times sound inconsequential to you? Well, according to ghost lore, these are the exact times that traditionally mark the arrival and departure of the spirits. Tie this in with the fact that people knew a séance room was being constructed right in the centre of the house, and you can begin to imagine the kind of gossip that circulated in the neighbourhood.

This séance room, otherwise known as the Blue Room, was supposedly where Sarah Winchester went every night in order to converse with the spirit world. There is a fascinating record of a visit from the great magician, escapologist and medium-debunker Harry Houdini. In 1924 he was in the area and stopped by the house for a tour and a midnight séance. Unfortunately there are no detailed records of what happened on the night of his visit.

In addition, the mansion is full of evidence of Sarah's obsession with the number 13, a number with many connections to superstition and the supernatural. In the guest reception hall there are thirteen ceiling panels, the house has thirteen bathrooms (the most recent of which boasts thirteen windows and thirteen steps leading to it), thirteen hooks in the séance room (to hold, it is said, the different robes worn by Sarah during her séances), thirteen holes in the drain covers and thirteen blue-and-amber jewels set into a spider-web window.

Perhaps unsurprisingly, then, given the house's background, ever since the 1920s there have been consistent reports of experiences of paranormal phenomena. According to one of the guidebooks on the house, visitors have gone temporarily blind and felt extreme drops in temperature. Other eyewitnesses have seen full-bodied apparitions in the basement or captured organ music on audio-recording equipment. As we know, the rumour mill was already in motion while Sarah Winchester was living in the house. When the doors were opened to the public after her death in 1922, visitors to its maze of rooms and architectural oddities, their appetite for strange occurrences surely already whetted by the stories surrounding it, immediately started to report the unusual experiences of which there are so many records. Their reports include sightings of apparitions, a sense of presence, temperature drops, light anomalies (i.e., light flashes or orbs with no apparent natural source) and auditory phenomena like mysterious footsteps, music and voices. More recently, an investigative group have reported experiencing banging sounds and a bizarre 'phantom smell'. Now it was our turn.

Our Investigation Begins

Ciarán: *We're just trying to get a feel for the place first. Normally with a big location it takes a couple of walk-rounds, preferably with a guide, to become accustomed with the layout. It is imperative to become extremely familiar with a location in daylight, so that if a night-time investigation is warranted you will feel confident moving around the space. Also, on an investigation it is useful to have access to floorplans so that you can highlight areas where phenomena have occurred or witnesses have experienced a potential haunting. With this location it is already a nightmare, and the lights aren't even off yet! There are no floorplans available and it will take more than a couple of tours for us to become familiar with this interior. There are a few rooms that are relatively normally furnished, in a dark-wood Victorian style, and they are quite welcoming. The rest of the house, though, is bare, which makes navigation very difficult. Many of the rooms and corridors look similar, and although in most large houses there is at least some logic applied to where stairs or corridors are, that definitely isn't the case here.*

Yvette: *This really is a maze. We're walking round with one of the guides and I can't get my head round the size or layout of this place. It is impossible to know what's around the next corner or what's behind any door. Even though it's the middle of the day and everywhere is quite bright I can already feel the spookiness of this place. The complex routes are unnerving, as are the bare plaster and floorboards of some rooms. It doesn't take much to imagine the shuffling figure of Sarah Winchester going from one room to the next, plotting her next architectural escape from the spirits. I must calm down. I'm already starting to imagine her eyes penetrating through some hidden spy-hole, watching our every move. God knows what I'll be like later tonight when the lights go out. What's that Ciarán just said? Time to go down to the haunted basement! Oh, why do we put ourselves through this!*

In the Haunted Basement

Yvette: *What a place to start. Earlier on, when we walked around in daylight, the basement was the only place that felt truly spooky to me. Now that the lights are off, for some reason Ciarán wants to start . . . in the basement! You have to watch your head stepping down here, it's a very low ceiling. Oh no, I don't like this at all. It's horrible. I remember what all this looked like when the lights were on and there were twists and turns and a couple of long corridors. Could be anything lurking round the corner. Right, stop it. Stay calm, get your rational hat on for a moment Yvette. Okay, that's it. Okay, so there's banging again. Ciarán and I discussed this earlier and the regular banging is known to have a plumbing source. That's been verified by other investigators. The irregular banging, though, could be paranormal. It's a slightly different sound from the regular noises. Let's try and establish contact. 'Is there anyone there? If there's someone there knock twice.' Nothing. Oops, there's one knock. Let's try again . . .*

Ciarán: *Given the sheer size of this building, it makes sense to have some plan of attack. So I suggest working from the basement up. I've already set up motion sensors in one of the kitchen areas and some audio equipment elsewhere. The motion sensors will sound an alarm should anything pass them and immediately begin sending footage to my laptop's hard drive. There are a couple* of mp3 recorders in the ballroom. I've had them there most of the day and will keep them running during our investigation. Baseline readings have already been logged. I've done cursory checks of temperature, EMF and other environmental variables throughout, then taken detailed readings in the more relevant parts of the house. For example, in the room known as Daisy's bedroom some people have reported icy-cold temperatures, so it makes sense to set up temperature data loggers there. Here in the basement the main phenomenon reported is the apparition of a man in overalls, along with a sense of presence. Infrasound could possibly explain the sense of presence, but the only environmental explanation for an apparition is EMF, so I've conducted a detailed survey here. Having examined the data, I think I may already have pinpointed an area where EMF levels may be responsible for people's experiences. I'm taking a different EMF meter down to the basement with me this time in order to verify my findings. Wow, it's dark!

A Séance

We stay for a while in the basement checking out the banging sounds. Yvette couldn't establish contact, and given that the knocks are so far apart, we're assuming that there's a natural explanation. Yvette thinks it may be from upstairs, either a door closing or a creaky floorboard that only makes a sound when someone walks across it. We can check that later. Back on the ground floor we venture through various rooms with stone floors. A quick check on the motion sensor set up in the kitchen reveals nothing. Ciarán makes a mental note to check the movements of the staff, as the back corridor is a main thoroughfare and even motion all the way back there could be picked up on the sensors. In the Morning Room the furnishings are lush and decadent and remind us very much of séance rooms we've seen in photos from the Spiritualism era. The circular wooden table looks perfect for a séance. Yvette is very keen to conduct one and so we ask medium David Wells to join us.

Yvette immediately starts reporting a temperature drop. The thermal imager isn't picking up a draft and the laser thermometer is registering a 1°C drop in Yvette's body temperature, which is a pretty small change. Ciarán quickly dispels any suggestion of a paranormal explanation and says it may well be because she is sitting still. David picks up on the presence of various characters in the house, including a female called Elizabeth, Sarah herself and a possibly Native American gentleman at her side. Yvette quizzes him as to whether this could be Sarah's spirit guide, but he's more inclined to think that it is a companion or servant. Ciarán suggests calling out in a language that the Native American spirit might understand.

Prior to our visit we had talked about the possibility that locations hold different layers of history. Not only do older buildings stand through various generations and historical changes, but they have also been built on land that may have a significant history of its own. In researching the Winchester Mystery House we had toyed with the possibility that we might encounter spirits of the missionaries who would have lived and worked in this area in times past, or the Native Americans whose land was in this part of America. The Native Americans who lived here would have been part of the larger nation of the Ohlone, with their smaller group being the Tamyen. It proved impossible for us to track down the language of the Tamyen as, in common with many Native American languages, it died out as the numbers of its speakers declined. However, Ciarán has been able to track down some words from the language spoken by the Mutsuns, who were also a subgroup of the Ohlone nation and were possibly neighbours to the Tamyen. Yvette and David repeat the words and phrases discovered by Ciarán, amongst them 'Mismin Tuuhis' or 'Hello', 'Tumsamiy kaan/Tumsanak kannis', which mean 'Please' and 'Thank you' and 'Hinka-me?' or 'What are you doing?'

There are a couple of creaks from underneath the table and Yvette is still saying that the temperature is dropping. Ciarán is still not getting a reading of a temperature drop to match Yvette's report, however; and Yvette and David say that they may have shifted their weight slightly, causing the creaks. Not having much success with the Mutsun language, David continues attempting to communicate, explaining that, for him, the 'language' by which he engages with spirits tends to be in the form of in images and symbols. Other mediums too, he explains, do not see language as a barrier to their communications with spirits.

Universal Language

We have both worked with a variety of mediums from various backgrounds, with differing beliefs and philosophies. Ciarán has spoken to literally hundreds of mediums in the course of his research. One question that comes up frequently is that of communicating with non-English-speaking spirits. Isn't it a problem? The argument frequently put forward by mediums is for a 'Universal Language'. This idea is akin to something called 'Adamic language', variations of which are found referenced in most religions. Adamic language is mentioned in the Biblical story of the Tower of Babel, and was supposedly the language spoken by Adam and Eve before they left the Garden of Eden. This 'Universal Language' that some mediums speak of would mean that there would be no communication problems for mediums who heard spirits talking in a language they didn't know. Indeed, Professor David Fontana, in his book *Is There an Afterlife?*, states, 'spirits are said to be able to use only the languages and the vocabulary that mediums already have in their heads.' Having said this, though, there are rare incidences of mediums communicating in foreign languages. For example, Etta Wriedt, an American medium investigated by scientists in the early 1900s, professed to only speak English but was reported, while communicating with spirits, to have spoken in Dutch, French, Spanish, Norwegian, Serbian, Croatian and Arabic!

We're excited by the first couple of hours of our investigation. Although the séance didn't result in any phenomena of note, the information about the Native American was interesting. We decide to continue alone, and make our way into the storeroom where millions of dollars worth of glass is kept; it was meant for windows that never made it into the building before Sarah died. We then head upstairs on what is called the 'Switchback Staircase'. This staircase has forty-four steps, but each one only rises a couple of inches. So, although there are seven complete turns and you walk around 100 feet, the staircase in fact takes you only nine feet higher than where you started! We then enter a series of rooms that are completely bare.

Yvette: *I'm glad to be out of the basement but that temperature drop during the séance was weird. I'm not keen on this area though. It's very bare, no decoration and no furniture of any kind. I daren't turn around too much in case I lose my bearings. We're in the dark and only have the light from this camcorder to guide us. I've got my torch but I don't want to switch it on – part of me likes the adrenalin rush of wandering round in the dark, not knowing what'll happen. What's in there? Some of these rooms have bizarre random cupboards and occasionally I'm surprised by hidden toilets or deceptive doors. I can see how visitors might get headaches or dizziness from the disorientation. I think it would be best if we continue heading up to the large, more open room that's surrounded by glass. If we do that then I'll have a better idea of where we are. We could also try some EVP (Electronic Voice Phenomena) work there.*

Ciarán: *I found the séance fascinating because it afforded me the opportunity to try out the Mutsun language. Didn't really work though. This is high given that normally the lightest reading in a domestic setting would be about 30mG next to various electronic appliances. Possibly that was a consequence of bad wiring, or at least wires that were not earthed. Now we're just walking around some of the upper levels. It's a little disconcerting up here as each room looks the same. Yvette wants to head upstairs and try some EVP. Now, where should we go? Nope, not that staircase, it goes nowhere!*

There are a couple of times on the way to the uppermost floor when we both think we see a shadow, but each time we realise that it's a trick of the light or a reflection from an unexpected window. We both tread carefully in every room we enter, keen to be extra-vigilant for any strange phenomena. We reach the top room, the north conservatory. It houses a unique floor system that in Sarah's day directed runoff water from the houseplants to the garden below. Yvette instructs Ciarán to grab his Dictaphone and try some EVP. We stand perfectly still, aware that any movement could be picked up by the microphone and easily misinterpreted later. Yvette calls out, leaving significant pauses between her questions to give spirits a chance to answer. It's only after asking a few questions and then playing them back that we think we may have caught something. There is a definite response to one set of questions. Ciarán suggests heading to Daisy's bedroom, where he has another laptop set up. We rush down there, barely able to control our excitement. Ciarán plays the sound file, saved on the laptop .

'Is there anybody here? Please can you talk to me?' Yvette's pleading voice rings in the air.

Silence for about five seconds.

'Please talk to me, let me know that you're here, tell me your name.'

A brief pause, then in hushed tones, 'Elizabeth.'

We look at each other in disbelief. David had mentioned a spirit called Elizabeth. This is unbeliev-able! Yvette can barely contain her excitement, although Ciarán is still exercising caution. This is potentially amazing evidence; we want to be sure. We need to play it for some other people and look into some of the possible rational or 'sceptical' explanations.

EVP and Pareidolia

EVP (Electronic Voice Phenomena), which has been around since the 1950s, gives us the most exciting and compelling evidence of alleged spirit communication. The theory of EVP is that with a recording device running in a 'haunted' location, you ask questions, as Yvette did in the Winchester Mystery House. Although nothing can be heard at the time, the device picks up voices and sounds not detectable to the ears of those listening. These sounds can be heard when the recording is played back later, as we experienced with the recording from Yvette's experiment.

Pareidolia is a term from mainstream psychology and is something to be aware of when dealing with EVP. It is the same effect as that which occurs when someone does a Rorschach inkblot test, which was mentioned earlier in the book. These are the tests that involve a psychologist presenting a patient with a series of cards featuring random patterns of inkblots and asking them what they see. Different patients come up with different ideas as to what the pictures are of – the Devil, a butterfly, etc – even though the patterns are all in fact abstract. The essence of the theory is that we human beings are hardwired to find patterns in randomness. Look up at the clouds and you see faces. Listen to the static on a radio and you'll hear voices. The same idea applies to EVP. If there is any noise to be heard, then it's possible, and indeed fairly likely, that the listener will find a pattern in the sounds and apply significance to it.

Conclusion

There is no doubt that this house has a serious paranormal history; the eyewitness accounts have been coming thick and fast for years. The exact motivation for Sarah's obsessive building and developing must remain a mystery, as must the issue of the 'family curse'. Remember Adam Coons, the Boston medium said to have confirmed her fears and counselled her to keep developing her house until the day she died? Ciarán has conducted extensive searches through records from Spiritualist churches and circles in the Boston area in the late 1800s, and has been unable to find any record of an Adam Coons. His part in Sarah Winchester's story makes for a compelling tale, there's no doubt about that, but with no evidence that he ever existed we must question the truth of the legend. There is no doubt, however, that the Winchester Mystery House lives up to its name, surrounded as it is by an aura of the strange and unexplained that seems to grow stronger with each passing year.

Ciarán: *Can I ever not be sceptical? I came here with a sceptical mind and I leave with answers, but I'm no closer to stepping off the fence onto Yvette's side. The answers I've found, though, are very exciting. In my opinion I've managed to find a viable rational explanation for the apparition seen in the basement (high levels of EMF), verify the rational explanation for the banging in the same location (plumbing), find a possible source for the bizarre smell in the ballroom (a wood-dominated kitchen nearby that may have absorbed and still be transmitting the 'ghosts' of all the cooking scents of its history) and enjoyed researching the Native American culture in the area. I found the EVP fascinating but I'm not convinced by it. We recorded the whole investigation on DV camcorders, and with the two recordings synced up it is possible that an ordinary human voice could have been misheard and misinterpreted as being of spirit origin. Yvette and I have argued about this and still can't agree! I'm happy to leave the question of its veracity open. Anyway, whether or not you are inclined to think that it was a ghostly voice, admit it – when you read the opening paragraph of this chapter, weren't you spooked?*

Yvette: *What do I think of the Winchester Mystery House? I loved it. What particularly intrigued me was the banging in the basement and the temperature drops, especially when we conducted that séance in the Morning Room. The whole building has such an* amazing atmosphere and being able to explore that maze-like layout at night was fantastic. Ciarán and I have argued constantly about the EVP and we've just got to agree to disagree! I think it's brilliant. In fact, I agree with many of the North American ghost groups who say that now EVP is where the most convincing evidence can be found. Well, I've witnessed it first-hand and I'm impressed. Overall, I think the Winchester Mystery House should remain a mystery that is never solved. It has an air of secrecy the moment you enter it, which is helped by the fabulously mystifying story behind its creation. Some mysteries were never meant to be solved, just to fascinate.

AFTERWORD: Belief in the paranormal

BELIEF AT HOME

The fans we meet at our book signings and live television events are walking proof of an increasing willingness to openly discuss paranormal experiences. Even just a few years ago there were hardly any TV shows around that concerned themselves with the paranormal. Compare that to the wealth of paranormal dramas, documentaries and reality-based shows on our screens now. And let's not forget the prevalence of blockbuster movies with paranormal themes, some of which exercise such a hold on the culture that lines from them have made their way into our vocabulary (Haven't you, at least once, whispered to someone 'I see dead people', probably the most famous line from M. Night Shyamalan's *The Sixth Sense*?)

There was a brief boom in public interest in the paranormal back in the early nineties, when Mulder and Scully of TV series *The X Files* for a time dominated popular culture. Our current level of interest over-shadows even *X Files* hysteria, though. The viewing ratings for TV shows concerned with the paranormal, the brimming shelves of the New Age sections in even mainstream high-street bookshops, the cult of the celebrity medium, and the popularity of ghost-themed movies and the related genre of horror, undoubtedly speak of the continuing rise in the public appetite for paranormal subjects.

These anecdotal observations are backed up by research. In 2005 a poll conducted for the *Sun* news-paper revealed that forty-three per cent of 1000 people surveyed believed that they had either been contacted by the dead or contacted the dead them-selves. Thirty-four per cent said they believed in ghosts, and thirty-seven per cent believed in restless spirits. Eighteen per cent had experienced tarot cards, sixteen per cent had visited psychics and another sixteen per cent had experienced palm-reading.

A very recent survey conducted online by Ann Winsper and Steve Parsons from the investigative group Para.Science showed a similarly high level of paranormal experiences and beliefs. At time of writing, the survey has received over 1800 responses, which raise some fascinating topics. These include a high percentage of respondents reporting not only that they have seen a ghost or apparition, but also that they believed the apparition to be aware of them.

AND ABROAD

In the USA, too, a recent survey has revealed fascinating things about the American people's beliefs in all areas of religion and spirituality. The Baylor Religion Survey, conducted in late 2005, questioned over 1700 Americans, not just on their religious beliefs and practices but also on topics such as astrology, alien visitation, telekinesis, UFOs, bizarre creatures and the phenomenon of forewarning of future events.

Of particular interest to us was the response to the statement 'Places can be haunted'. A whopping 37.2% agreed. Additionally, 12.5% had had experience with a psychic, medium or similar figure, 21.5% said they had had a haunting experience, and 7.5% reported experience with a ouija board.

As we discuss in the section of this book where our investigations take us across the Channel to France, we started out feeling that belief in the paranormal was less widespread in France than it is in the UK and the USA. In a way we still think that this is true; the subject certainly does not seem to attract the same level of media coverage in France as is the norm in the two other countries. However, although some of the people we spoke to while investigating in France were reticent about sharing their beliefs and experiences with us, we did still manage to unearth plenty of fascinating, if not downright hair-raising, stories.

Maybe the culture in France is still to keep your beliefs on the paranormal to yourself. Because the UK is currently riding a huge wave of public interest and belief in paranormal issues, it is easy to forget that this is a very recent phenomenon; interest and media coverage has only really undergone a dramatic rise in the UK over the last decade. Perhaps France is poised for a similar surge in popularity. Watch this space!

THE POPULAR PARANORMAL

Judging by the arresting statistics we have looked at, from both home and abroad, interest and belief in the paranormal is definitely on the increase. What might be responsible for this huge surge of public interest?

One theory is that disillusionment with our modern lives and society is leading more and more of us to investigate alternatives, including the paranormal. There may be a religious aspect too. The paranormal is sometimes described as the 'new religion'. Perhaps people are rejecting mainstream religion, feeling that it does not deliver the answers or experiences they are seeking. Yvette certainly believes this, feeling that some people find their answers in the paranormal. Ciarán, sounding a note of caution, thinks that there is a phenomenon of what he calls 'fast-food' religion, whereby a person might come out of an experience like one visit to a medium feeling that their questions have been answered and they have all the evidence they need to confirm their beliefs.

What about modern science? Some studies suggest that certain paranormal experiences can be explained away by the makeup of an individual's brain chemistry. Groundbreaking studies in Canada found that the level of an individual's temporal lobe lability (the amount of electrical activity in the brain) may go at least some way towards explaining phenomena like alien abduction and experiences of seeing or otherwise sensing ghosts and other 'haunting' phenomena. It is also possible for a person to undergo a partial complex seizure (a brain seizure) without being aware of it; this could also explain why some people experience strange phenomena.

Recent research in London has also succeeded in replicating out-of-body experiences (OBEs), which some have interpreted as a natural, rational explanation to do with brain function.

These investigations and others like them, then, to a point seem to be turning the tide of belief towards rationality and against proof of the existence of the paranormal. Fascinatingly, though, there is another side to this coin. The application of mainstream science to matters paranormal may in some cases be casting doubt on them, but there is traffic in the other direction too; investigators into the paranormal are increasingly applying mainstream science to their experiments and investigations. Many contemporary published works on the paranormal are using the language of science, notably quantum physics and its application to paranormal phenomena.

There is also a noticeable trend towards complementing laboratory-based study with phenomenological, or experience-focused, work. More and more parapsychologists are going into the field (haunted houses or séance circles, for example) to witness people's beliefs and activities at first hand.

This coming together of mainstream science and other ways of working and investigating is an important tool in the ongoing mission to answer the question of why it is that human belief in the paranormal exists. And if we ever do answer that question it would, to borrow from Stephen Hawking, be the ultimate form of self-discovery – for then we should know the mind of God.

Some final thoughts

We are incredibly grateful to be working at this point in time, with interest in the paranormal, and the demand for answers, at an all-time high. This interest and demand convinces us that there is a huge need for paranormal investigators like us, to keep pushing the boundaries and searching and searching for the answers we all seek. And as long as people continue to want answers, we will keep working, searching, and carrying out our investigations.

We both thoroughly enjoyed the investigations in this book, which as you have learned, took place in some pretty wild and frequently classically 'spooky' settings. After the atypical haunted locations of the first book, we found ourselves irresistibly drawn to these eerie castles and creepy tunnel systems. We both had a 'dream-come-true' experience – for Ciarán the investigation of Dartford Library and for Yvette our night-time experience of Anne Boleyn's home Hever Castle. All of these investigations, though, were an adventure and a privilege. They reminded us that, although we are now seasoned ghost hunters, there is always more to learn and more to experience. They also reminded us of how lucky we are to have such an amazing job; to be able to spend our time following our passion for the paranormal, in the hope that one day we will find our very own Holy Grail: scientific proof of the existence of ghosts. Until that day comes, we will continue our adventure and our journey into the unknown. If you continue to support us and follow our progress, there's no saying where it might eventually take us all!

APPENDIX A:
Investigative Groups, Societies & Sites of Interest

The authors do not endorse any ghost group and are not in any way liable for the behaviour of a group during an investigation unless they are personally in attendance. For those interested in seeking a group to join, or to invite for an investigation, the authors recommend enquiring via national organisations such as the SPR or ASSAP.

THE GHOST CLUB

The Ghost Club was founded in 1862, and is the oldest organisation in the world associated with psychical research. Their prime interest is that of paranormal phenomena associated with ghosts and hauntings.

WEBSITE: www.ghostclub.org.uk

SOCIETY FOR PSYCHICAL RESEARCH (SPR)

The purpose of the SPR is to advance the understanding of events and abilities commonly described as 'psychic' or 'paranormal', without prejudice and in a scientific manner.

WEBSITE: www.spr.ac.uk
(American Society for Psychical Research www.aspr.com)

THE ASSOCIATION FOR THE SCIENTIFIC STUDY OF ANOMALOUS PHENOMENA (ASSAP)

An association dedicated to discovering the scientific truth behind unexplained anomalous phenomena. ASSAP has no corporate beliefs and encourages an open-minded, undogmatic scientific approach to its subject.

WEBSITE: www.assap.org

THE PARAPSYCHOLOGIST (Dr. Ciarán O'Keeffe)

Provides information about parapsychology. The aim is to disseminate information, to expose the facts and let you decide.

WEBSITE: www.theparapsychologist.com

THE DERBYSHIRE PEAKS

A site put together by Derbyshire County Council's Libraries and Heritage Department, The British Library and Peak District National Park Authority.

WEBSITE: www.peaklandheritage.org.uk

FORTEAN TIMES

The world of strange phenomena all found in a comprehensive website and addictive magazine. Ciarán subscribes to it anyway!

WEBSITE: www.forteantimes.com

APPARITIONS OF BLACK DOGS

Website detailing Dr Simon Sherwood's research into Black Dogs.

WEBSITE: www.blackshuck.info

APPENDIX B:
Recommended Reading and Viewing

The following are sources that Yvette and Ciarán either found useful during their research or are directly referenced in the book.

BOOKS AND WEBSITES

Baigent, M., Leigh, R. & Lincoln, H., *The Holy Blood & The Holy Grail*, London: Jonathan Cape, 1982.

Cotton, C., *The Genuine Poetical Works of Charles Cotton*, London: R. Bonwicke, 1715, 2007.

Dozier Jr., R. W., *Fear Itself: The origin and nature of the powerful emotion that shapes our lives and our world*, New York: Thomas Dunne Books, 1999.

Fontana, D., *Is There An Afterlife?*, London: O Books, 2005.

Gauld, A., *Mediumship and Survival: A century of*

investigations, London: Heinemann, 1982.

Hines, T., *Pseudoscience and the Paranormal: A critical examination of the evidence*, Buffalo, NY: Prometheus Books, 1987, 2002.

O'Keeffe, C., 'Interviewing eyewitnesses in spontaneous cases: The need for a Cognitive Interview style'. Paper presented at the 25th International Conference of the Society for Psychical Research, Clare College, Cambridge, 2001.

Roux, J., Brenon, A. & Jachowicz-Davoust, B., *The Cathars*, Vic-en Bigorre, France: MSM Editions, 2006.

Slemen, T., *Haunted Liverpool 12*, Liverpool: Bluecoat Press, 2006.

Stonehouse, J., *The Streets of Liverpool*, Liverpool: Hime & Sons, 1869, 2002.

Stuart, N. R., *The Reluctant Spiritualist: The life of Maggie Fox,* Florida, USA: Harcourt, Inc., 2005.

Tyrell, G. N. M., *Apparitions*, London: SPR, 1953, 1973.

Underwood, P., *Ghosts and how to see them*, London: Anaya Publishers Ltd., 1994.

Wiseman, R., Watt, C., Greening, E., Stevens, P. and O'Keeffe, C., 'An investigation into the alleged haunting of Hampton Court Palace: Psychological variables and magnetic fields', *Journal of Parapsychology*, 66(4), 2002, pp387-408.

www.skepdic.com (The Sceptic's Dictionary)

FILMS AND TV

In the first book we listed a number of our favourite scary films (though Yvette still won't watch *The Exorcist*!). Here we add some more, and also expand the list to include films and TV that deal with other aspects of the paranormal like psychokinesis, and other ghostly TV favourites.

Afterlife (TV series)
Carrie (1976)
Don't Look Now (1973)
Ghost of Mae Nak (2005)
Kairo (2001)
The Changeling (1980)
The Innocents (1961)
The Stone Tape (1972 TV movie)
Shutter: They Are Around Us (2004)

ACKNOWLEDGEMENTS

FROM CIARÁN & YVETTE

As this second chapter of unchartered supernatural discovery closes, there are those who served as explorers' aids, without whom some adventures would never have transpired:

To Richard Davidson and the wonderful staff at Dartford Library, the Liverpool City Council (Parks Estates), Park Rangers and Tom Slemen for pointing the way to Allerton Tower, to Ann Watt for opening such welcoming doors to Hever Castle, for entrusting us with the keys to Stanley Palace, Janet Jones, to Mr Harrison and the indispensable guides at Speedwell and Peak Cavern (especially Gary's perfectly timed hot chocolate!), to Ruth Gordon and the Peakland Heritage site for creating such inspiring words, for allowing us into the darkest depths of Liverpool, the

Williamson Tunnels Heritage Centre and Friends of Williamson's Tunnels, to the Winchester mansion for letting us have a peek at its mystery, to the commune of Lapradelle-Puilaurens and the staff themselves at Château de Puilaurens for allowing us to 'prenez votre temps'. Merçi beaucoup and thank you very much.

Thank you also to those who selflessly provided propitious clues that helped map the route, Stuart Harrison and Lesley Smith. Thank you to David Wells for his invaluable spiritual presence in Dartford Library and the Winchester Mystery House. Thank you to those technical 'deckhands' who picked up the 'gauntlet' (i.e. DV camera) and helped immensely: Gaëlle Villejoubert; Stuart Torevell; Karl Beattie. This record of exploration would not exist in its present form were it not for Guy Rose, Nicola Doherty and Hannah Knowles and all those at Hodder & Stoughton who have supported it from the first mention of *Ghost Hunters*.

FROM CIARÁN

When an alleged haunting experience is reported, my response remembers Bob Morris and Maurice Grosse and, in this life, my sceptical voice echoes the influential knowledge of mentors Richard Wiseman and Laurence Alison. To my 'sister-in-arms', Yvette and her inimitable husband, Karl. To Mum and Dad for nurturing an academic. To the usual gang that hang out in the ship's galley ensuring that I'll always eat and drink well along the way and are there to listen, to my friends: Neal & Sharon; Emma Greening; Ian Baker; Andy Rose; The Professor. Not forgetting the Wycombe crowd who were there on the days it all really started. And finally: Time has told me you're a rare, rare find ... and I keep on finding the only thing supernatural in my life is how I ever found you. I love you Pretty.

FROM YVETTE

There are those who have been with me throughout this journey of the paranormal, without whose support and love I'd not be where I am today: To my paranormal sidekick and adopted bro Ciarán: you're the best. To my wonderful husband Karl and my two fantastic children, William and Mary: I love you. My Grandfather, 'Pops', who I am so proud of and who has always supported me. And for my mum, Angela, for being so brave and for being there.